READ YOUR BIBLE FOR REVIVAL

Awaken your first love,
enjoy fresh desire and
transform your life.

KIM MARTIN

Dear Carol,
Thank you for your support & friendship –
Lots of love
Kim Martin.

READ YOUR BIBLE FOR REVIVAL
Awaken your first love, enjoy fresh desire
and transform your life.

Copyright ©2012 by Kim Martin.
All rights reserved. No part of this publication may be used or reproduced in any matter whatsoever without written permission from the author, except in brief quotations written, recorded or spoken.

Contact the author – Kim Martin via email
kim@ReadYourBibleForRevival.org

All Scripture references are taken from the Amplified Bible unless otherwise stated at the point of reference.

Graphic design and artwork: Richard Martin.

ISBN-13: 978-1492365471
ISBN-10: 1492365475

THANK YOU...

… Holy Spirit, this book would not exist without You. You took Your precious Word and used it to awaken me in spirit and transform me, then You taught me how You did it. You gave me this teaching and now I write it as a monument of worship to You.

… Friends who encouraged me, I would not have fought through to continue writing this book without you. Especially Adele, Dawn, Yvette, Lisa, Richard, Hilary and Pastor Desmond. Your encouragement spurred me on.

… Family and friends who encouraged me and gave me their precious time, I would have despaired of ever completing this book without you. Especially Arron and Sammi, Tom and Wyn, Jan and Charlotte, Carol, Ugochi and Fiona.

… Monique, this book would be a pamphlet without you. You have been one of my biggest enthusiasts, keeping me going, drawing so much more out of me, giving me time and many sacrificial hours of editing.

… And finally Richard (my darling husband), this book would not exist without you. We share this journey and the cost of walking it out. You have transformed my writings into such a beautiful book.

I love and appreciate you all.

READING GUIDE
TO THE FOUR SECTIONS OF EACH CHAPTER

Bible study is vital; however, the thought of daily Bible study is overwhelming for most of us, who are busy and tired. This book bridges the gap between theology and everyday Christianity. Let the teaching and testimony in this book inspire and equip you to get started on a truly exciting and life changing relationship with God in and through His Word.

- *Teaching:* Each chapter begins with a biblically rich and very practical teaching section. Written to empower you with fresh biblical perspectives, practical ideas and motivation.
- *Testimony:* The teaching is followed by a portion of my testimony that pertains to the preceding teaching. Written to enrich the teaching with a personal story and inspire you.
- *Prayer:* Use this section as a spring board to vocalize your own response to God in the light of what you have read.
- *Commitment:* This book requires action so each chapter ends with a section for you to write out how you will act upon what you have read. It is an agreement between you and God. Write out how you will respond and commit your decision to God for His grace to help.

I would love to hear how you get on, or answer any questions. Email me at kim@ReadYourBibleForRevival.org or visit www.ReadYourBibleForRevival.org

CONTENTS

INTRODUCTION   9

ONE
READ TO FEED   11

TWO
HUNGER NEEDS DESIRE   25

THREE
CARVE OUT THE TIME   43

FOUR
READ ITS FULLNESS   59

FIVE
YOUR ULTIMATE LIFE COACH   77

SIX
THE FLESH   99

SEVEN
LIVING OUT YOUR PURPOSE   125

CONCLUSION   137

INTRODUCTION

Reading your Bible with an open and receptive heart is essential for spiritual vitality and supernatural living. Without regularly feeding your spirit the nutritional Word of God, you will be spiritually weak and ineffective.

I lived a lukewarm Christianity for most of my Christian life with no hope of ever living any differently. Then one day, confronted by my spiritual impotency, I decided to read my Bible cover to cover. As I did, my life changed forever.

By simply reading (not studying) my Bible, I found myself on a pilgrimage to the very heart of God. The fruit of this pilgrimage being the enjoyment of fresh intimacy with God, a real, vibrant and tangible connection with the Holy Spirit, spiritual zeal, faith, clarity of purpose, prophetic openness, unity in spirit with other Christians, a greater capacity for worship and prayer, and a heart to reach out to others; all in increasing measure.

The whole experience deepened my love for God, increased my capacity for intimate worship and transformed me from the inside out. I began to receive the spirit and life that flows from God's Word, experience its life-transforming power and live a renewed Christianity.

In this book, I share with you biblical perspectives and principles that paint a fresh picture on your relationship with your Bible. With biblically rich teaching and powerful testimony, I inspire and equip you to know God as intimately as you desire. Apply this teaching to your Bible reading, and your life will be radically transformed by the living, breathing book that is God Himself.

Majestic
Lord Jesus,
I need the wholesome
nourishment of Your
Word, to **live touching**
the **spiritual resources**
of the eternal
world.

Adapted from Hebrews 6:4 J.B. Phillips

ONE

READ TO FEED

READING YOUR BIBLE IS ESSENTIAL
FOR SPIRITUAL VITALITY

God intends Christianity to be simply powerful; our simple faith in His great power.[1] However, we rarely find it that simple, due to our continued wrestle with the tensions between our spirit and flesh.[2] This wrestle exists within the soul, from which you reason, desire and feel emotions.[3] It is the heart of you, caught between the leading of your temporal body and your eternal spirit.[4] This combination creates a tension in you of trying to manage living according to two realms. The lower natural realm, where you rely on your natural reasoning and physical senses, and the higher supernatural realm, where you rely on the Word of God and your spiritual senses.[5]

Despite the influence of your flesh, the true eternal you is spirit. So your innate longings are to live according to the higher supernatural realm. The realm of intimately knowing and loving God; walking through life hand-in-hand with His Holy Spirit and experiencing His kingdom come as part of your daily living. Unfortunately, these spiritual desires are quenched when your five flesh senses and natural thinking dominate how you think and, therefore, act.[6] The consequence is living subject to the natural realm with mere hints and glimpses of God and His miraculous ways.

---

[1] John 14:12 [2] 1 Thessalonians 5:23 [3] Psalm 103:1 and Mark 12:30 [4] Romans 7:22-24
[5] Mark 8:35 [6] Romans 8:8

Your ability to live according to the higher supernatural realm depends on the measure that you invest in the vitality of your spirit. This is because when you sow to your spirit, you reap of the Spirit but when you sow to your flesh, you reap of the flesh.[7] Whichever is dominantly fed and nurtured within you will be more acutely alive to influence how you interpret your world and live.

So how strong are you spiritually? Are you vibrant with spiritual thinking and actions? Take a few moments to consider the following questions as a simple self-evaluation;[8] ask yourself 'Do I…'

✦ Give intentional consideration to my spiritual health and strength?

✦ Have clarity of spiritual sight, hearing, discernment and purpose?

✦ Have a heart enthusiastically overflowing with worship throughout the week?

✦ Find prayer prophetic, enjoyable and refreshing?

✦ Have fresh revelation to easily and naturally share with others?

✦ Have current testimonies of what God is doing in, through and for me?

✦ Experience supernatural solutions to natural problems?

✦ Feel intimately connected to God as my heavenly Father?

✦ Understand and experience the presence of God and His ways in increasing measure over the weeks, months and years of my Christian life?

✦ Experience God unfolding His plans and purposes in and through me?

[7] Galatians 6:8   [8] 2 Corinthians 13:5

Before reading my Bible the way I do now, I would have said 'no' to many of the questions above. I was frustrated by my spiritual impotency, but felt helpless to do anything about it. However, since reading my Bible the way I do now, I have learned how to be spiritually strong and healthy, to enjoy intimacy with God, true spiritual fellowship with other Christians and a growing capacity for higher supernatural living. To my surprise, it was much simpler than I thought. I simply read my Bible as a spiritual book with my spiritual senses for my spiritual vitality.

In this book, I will teach you how to read your Bible to feed your spirit, so that it can rise up within you and lead you in connecting with the Holy Spirit. To then flow with Him as He teaches you how to truly live the Christian life. This is not a reading plan; this is a lifestyle of building intimacy with God and bearing fruit in life by abiding in His Word.[9] I will present perspectives of the Bible that can take it from being a book that you feel you should read, to being a book that you cannot live without.

IT ALL COMES BY A SPIRIT TO HOLY SPIRIT CONNECTION

If you are living life dominated by the senses and reasoning of your flesh, you will miss connecting with much of what God has planned to do in, for and through you supernaturally. If you have an awareness of what God wants to do in and through you, or you dare to dream big in God, then the natural restrictions that you experience will probably cause frustration and perhaps hopelessness. This is because God is Spirit,[10] and therefore living life His supernatural way depends on a vital connection to His Holy Spirit. Flesh connects with flesh and spirit connects with Holy Spirit.

Some time ago, my daughter and I were driving in our car when she said, "Look mummy, an aeroplane; lets catch it." I replied,

---

[9] John 15:1-10 [10] John 4:24

"We cannot catch it because cars drive on the ground and aeroplanes fly in the sky. No matter how hard I push the pedal, our car will never reach the heights of that plane." This got me thinking; the reason my Christian living has been so frustratingly limited is because I have been trying to connect with God, who is Spirit, with my flesh. Sadly no matter how hard I tried, I continually missed the connection and lived below the heights that He has planned for me.

You cannot pray, worship, love, fellowship, minister and serve as God intends in the sense and reasoning of your flesh. To live and love like God, you must do it with spiritual understanding and empowerment.[11] Your flesh is hostile to God and cannot submit itself to God's ways of living. However, your spirit is created to connect and flow with His Holy Spirit.[12]

For much of my Christian life I have misunderstood and neglected the needs of my spirit, but continually pandered to the demands of my flesh. Consequently, my flesh had been dominant in strength and was leading me in living my life.[13] I was 'flesh sensitive', but 'spiritually numb'. In recognizing that my spirit was weak while my flesh was strong, I decided to start feeding my spirit to revive it back to health and strength; to tip the balance in favor of empowering my spirit. My starting point was to realize my need for the essential spiritual nourishment of God's Word.

GOD'S WORD IS ESSENTIAL SPIRITUAL FOOD

In a state of extreme physical hunger and facing temptation to turn stones into bread, Jesus made a differentiation between natural food and spiritual food.[14] Feeding only our physical bodies is not sufficient; we also need to feed on God's Word for spiritual vitality. Jesus made this very clear when He said, *"Man shall not live and be sustained by (on) bread alone but by every word and expression of God."*[15] The author of Hebrews also likened dependence on natural

---

[11] Romans 8:4-13 [12] Matthew 26:41 and Romans 7:18 [13] Romans 8:8 [14] Deuteronomy 8:3
[15] Luke 4:4

food to feeding on the Word of God when he wrote, 'First we are nurtured on the milk of the Word but in time we must be weaned on to solid food and grow up'.[16] If a baby is limited to milk beyond weaning age, he will fail to thrive and it is the same for you with your spiritual diet. Are you developing your diet and getting the continual nutrients that you need to mature and thrive? Or are you living on a limited spiritual diet that is causing you to remain spiritually stunted? Are you relying on pastors and teachers to spoon-feed you with the spiritual food that they have already cut up, eaten and digested themselves? Godly preaching and teaching is vital for advancing the kingdom and training the body of Christ. However, part of maturing is learning how to feed yourself.

YOU NEED TO FEED YOURSELF TO THRIVE

The author of Hebrews further identifies the importance of the Word of God as the essential ingredient for maturing spiritually in writing, *"When you find men who have been enlightened, who have experienced salvation and received the Holy Spirit, who have known the wholesome nourishment of the Word of God and touched the spiritual resources of the eternal world…"*[17]

Just as above, I was enlightened in 1992 when I saw my need for Christ. I then experienced His gift of salvation and received the Holy Spirit. Then I desired to move on to touching the spiritual resources of the eternal world, but I just kept coming up short; why? Because I was trying to skip over the next step, 'to know and keep knowing the wholesome nourishment of the Word of God'. I wasn't feeding on the Word of God, so I remained spiritually malnourished, weak and impotent.

Imagine a person who has been lost in the desert… in the wilderness of dust and heat for days without food or water. When discovered, they are found lying almost lifeless, parched, scorched

---

[16] Hebrews 5:11-13 [17] Hebrews 6:4-8 JB Phillips

and malnourished; hardly able to lift their head or hand; their cry for food and water so faint you can barely hear it. Deep within me, my spirit had been making a similar desperate cry for attention. Unfortunately, I couldn't respond, as I didn't know how. So I struggled on, neglecting my deep need for essential spiritual nourishment to be spiritually revived.

However, once I connected the dots, I began to see that I was spiritually weak. In order to become spiritually strong, I needed to begin with feeding my malnourished spirit back to vitality. So I began reading my Bible regularly, with increasing bulk to nourish and build up my spiritual strength.

READING TO FEED

All that was required to motivate me to keep reading my Bible was this new perspective. Previously I had viewed my Bible as a big, hard-to-understand-and-apply historical book. I thought I had to intellectually study it to understand it and I thought I had to memorize it and repeat verses as a way of meditating on it. This perspective was blocking me from reading and enjoying my Bible. It all seemed too hard, time consuming and, quite frankly, boring. I had known the power of reading my Bible as a new Christian, but the passion and enthusiasm had long since been worn away. I knew selected portions of my Bible very well, but I rarely ever read it.

Changing my perspective to seeing my Bible as spiritual food meant that it was no longer optional for me. It became absolutely essential to read it for my spiritual life and vitality. So I started at Genesis and simply read. I laid aside any concern for memorizing, intellectualizing or studying my Bible to simply *read to feed*.

Reading to feed requires a posture of faith. Jesus said, *"It shall be done for you as you have believed."*[18] What you come to your Bible for, you will get. Approach it as the Tree of Knowledge and you will get

[18] Matthew 8:13

knowledge. However, approach it as the Tree of Life and you will get life, which includes knowledge.[19] Simply read and keep reading, with a believing expectation that the Word is going in to feed, nourish and strengthen you. When you eat a meal, you take it into your mouth, enjoy its taste and then swallow it down into your s=ach. Only then can its nutrients permeate and nourish your body. If you ate it just for the taste, chewing and chewing but not swallowing, you would experience the taste but miss out on the energy and nutrients. Likewise, if you limit the Word of God to mere information, you, in a sense, hold it captive in your intellect. Therefore failing to absorb, enjoy and benefit from its spirit and Life.

As you *read to feed*, take in the words and allow them to flow through your mind and drop down into your spirit. I am not suggesting that you switch your brain off as you read. Rather, embrace the reality that there is more to reading your Bible than a mere intellectual exchange. The Bible is different from any other book as it is more than just print on pages. Jesus is the Word[20] and His words are spirit and life.[21] The Bible is the living, breathing, active Word of God.[22] As you continually behold it and gaze into it, you will be transfigured into the likeness of Christ in ever increasing splendor and from one degree of glory to another.[23]

As you *read to feed* imagine this:

- ✦ Your eyes, ears or fingertips functioning like your lips and taking in the food.
- ✦ Your intellect functioning like your mouth-chewing, breaking down and tasting the food.
- ✦ Your spirit functioning like your stomach and intestines – digesting and distributing the nutrition and energy to your whole being, which is, spirit, soul and body.

[19] Genesis 2:9 [20] John 1:14 [21] John 6:63 [22] Hebrews 4:12 [23] 2 Corinthians 3:18

As you read your Bible to digest its spirit and life, you will receive its vital nutrition and energy:

+ Its nutrition: The pure teaching that renews your mind, so that you increasingly think like God and embrace His supernatural perspectives.
+ Its energy: A force that causes a vibrant passion for God and His ways to flourish within you.

When you continually *read to feed,* your spirit will become nourished and energized to rise up within you to lead you in making a spirit to Holy Spirit connection. Given time, your spirit will rise up sufficiently to tip the balance in favor of living for the things of the Spirit above living for things of the flesh. Then as you nurture and respond to your spiritual revival, you will come alive and burn passionately for the things of God. Then reading your Bible, praying, worshipping and reaching out will become irresistible to you.

Reading to feed is just the beginning. However, it is an essential foundation for spiritual maturity to touch the spiritual resources of His eternal world in a stable and sustainable way.

MY TESTIMONY

In 1996, as a relatively new Christian and wife, I was completely broken from years of abuse. I couldn't bear being alive, but was unable to take my own life because of my responsibilities to my precious young son. Unable to find any help, healing or escape, I was desperate and without hope. Then I read an old second hand book about reading the Bible cover to cover, and I was inspired to give it a go. As I read from Genesis to Revelation, I discovered God as my Heavenly Father. I fell head over heels in love with Him and

His Word. From this, I enjoyed a growing capacity to sit in His presence and simply receive. I would sit for hours with no agenda, but to enjoy and love Him. I would sing portions of worship songs, pray (in English and in tongues), but mostly I would sit in silence. By simply reading my Bible, my priorities changed. Just like Mary (sister of Martha and Lazarus),[24] I began giving first place to sitting in God's presence ahead of my obligation to serving others. Then as I did, He used His Word and presence to reach into my heart and mend the brokenness. By the end of a year, I wanted to live again and I had hope and purpose for my life and my marriage. There was more healing to come, but the transformation in that year was miraculous and I was in a healthier place to serve.

Then as time went on, I became busy and gave up reading my Bible; consequently the intimacy was lost. On the surface I was a 'good' Christian. I was committed and active in church, listening to hours and hours of preaching and quoting Scriptures, but my heart had grown lukewarm. No matter what I tried, I could not get back to enjoying reading my Bible or the intimacy that I had enjoyed with God. I resigned myself to the fact that this intimacy was a 'special anointed gift' for that desperate season in my life. While confronted with the possibility that I would never experience such a love affair with God again, deep down I still yearned for it.

Then one day in 2011, I joined with Christian friends to pray for a sick child; one after the other we asked God to heal the child. The expectations were low and any sense that 'we could have whatever we ask for in prayer, believing that it is granted to us,'[25] was missing. This event effected me and I was jolted by how little faith and expectancy there was. Feeling fed up with a powerless Christianity, I stated to myself and my husband that, 'either God and His Word are real, or they aren't.' It was do-or-die for me. I wanted to give it one last shot to make Christianity real, or I would walk away from it all. I had given my heart, time and money to

[24] Luke 10:39-42 [25] Mark 11:23-25

Christianity, as I understood it, for years and yet felt spiritually bankrupt and impotent.

So I decided to rise one hour earlier each day and read my Bible cover to cover. To my delight, within a matter of weeks I started to experience the same connections that I had felt in 1996. However, this time the focus was conviction and refining, rather than heart healing.

Although God's focus has been different each time, the experience of being revived is very much the same. My spiritual senses and desires rose up within me and connected me with the Holy Spirit. God became increasingly real to me and I fell passionately in love with Him all over again. As my spiritual senses were regenerating, I began hearing the Holy Spirit speak to me from His written Word with clarity. Revelation was beginning to flow and I was being transformed. I realized that the transformation came from reading my Bible consistently and in bulk, so I continued. Then as I did, the Holy Spirit taught me the mechanics behind what I was experiencing, so that I could maintain it and share it. *Reading to feed* has become vital to me, and will continue to be for the rest of my life.

As a busy mum, I like to treat my *reading to feed* time as 'me time'. It is the time that I care for and nurture the real me, and it has become so precious to me. My favorite way to read my Bible is to get a cup of coffee, put on some 'soaking' worship, curl up and enjoy immersing myself. I find that soaking in an environment of worship enhances my communion with the Holy Spirit as I read His Word.

Understanding the simplicity of *reading to feed* lifted any pressure. I can simply read, trusting that the Word is going in and doing a great work, no matter how I feel. Even when I am tired or fed up, I can read, because all I have to do is relax and have a good feed. If I don't feel like reading my Bible, or my intellect isn't enjoying it, I simply tell my soul, "Kim, your spirit needs this; just feed." Because I was so malnourished and hungry, I decided to bulk feed to see results fast. I began feeding, loved it and kept going, and read my Bible cover to cover in 13 weeks.

My experiences and new perspectives have instilled in me an absolute dependency on my Bible for my spiritual health and strength. I have only scratched the surface of being spiritually alive and discovering God as my first love. I never want to go back to the dullness of being lukewarm again.

ACTION STEPS

+ Choose a version that you can enjoy reading through. I enjoyed starting with the Cover-to-Cover Complete edition because it is chronological and interspersed with little devotional sections. As this is a life long journey, you will probably read many translations over the years.

+ Maintain the faith posture that you are *reading to feed* your spirit. If you think you are finding your Bible boring or hard to read, keep reading whilst telling yourself, "I am feeding." In the following chapters, I will teach you how to build on *reading to feed* by connecting and receiving, which is what makes Bible reading and Christian living really exciting.

+ Don't be too concerned about what effect the Word is having on your intellect. At this stage, read the words to put them in, trusting that they are dropping into your spirit to nourish your whole being spirit, body and soul; just like food passes through your mouth to reach your stomach and into your blood stream.

+ Free yourself from pressure to memorize, meditate or study. It is the role of the Holy Spirit to teach you and bring the Word to your remembrance. I will teach this in more detail in Chapter five.

- ✦ Bulk feeding is required to revive your spirit; a daily verse or reading a book that contains Scripture will have little effect. The more of the Word you can put in, the more benefit you will feel in your spirit and the more encouraged you will be to keep going.

- ✦ Give the Word time to take effect; nourishing a malnourished spirit to health will take time. You need to counterbalance a prolonged famine of the pure, written, nourishing Word with a prolonged feast.

- ✦ Develop your own pace, striking a balance between pushing yourself yet being kind to yourself. Given time and bulk, discipline will turn into enthusiastic devotion.

- ✦ Be consistent; a prolonged personal, spiritual revival requires regular (daily) feeding.

PRAYER

Father God, I am sorry for neglecting Your Word and my spiritual needs. I didn't realize how important my Bible was. Thank You for such a miracle that by simply reading my Bible I can be spiritually revived. Father God, lead me in choosing which version to read. Help me to receive its nutrition and help me to patiently persist in *reading to feed*, while expectantly waiting to experience the reviving results. Amen.

PERSONAL COMMITMENT

Now I see that I am an eternal spiritual being and that the Word of God is vital nutrition for my spiritual health and strength, to connect with God and His higher ways, I commit to…

....
....
....
....
....
....
....
....

Wonderful
Lord Jesus,
I open my mouth and taste, open my eyes and see, how good You are.
I am blessed when I run to You.

Adapted from Psalm 34:8 The Message

TWO
HUNGER NEEDS DESIRE
OUR APPETITES DRIVE US IN LIFE

What you hunger for physically, emotionally and spiritually, you pursue.[1] Depending on the severity of your hunger, you may look forward to a satisfying indulgence, or you may be consumed by the thought of what you need with an urgent desperation. Esau was so hungry for food that he exchanged his birthright for a bowl of stew.[2] The exchange seems extreme, but he believed that he was about to die from his hunger, so food was all he could think of.

The pangs of physical hunger are obvious, but what about emotional or spiritual hunger? What are you satisfying your hunger for love, acceptance, purpose, meaning and knowing God with? There is the old saying, 'we all have a God shaped hole in our heart that only God can fill, but we spend our lives trying to fill it with so many other things'. What are you filling your emotional and spiritual hunger with? TV, media, people, career or something else? What are you putting ahead of reading your Bible, worshipping and praying on a regular basis?

You are created to be hungry for the things that you need as a prompting to survive and thrive. This includes an innate hunger for God and therefore His Word. If you feel hungry for food, you know what to do about it: get some food and eat. But what if you didn't enjoy food? You would struggle to motivate yourself to eat, and it is just the same with your emotional and spiritual needs. If reading your Bible, praying and worshipping are not desirable to you, then

---

[1] Proverbs 16:26 [2] Genesis 25:29-34

you will struggle to find the motivation. You will use more desirable substitutes that satisfy your flesh, rather than your spirit to suppress the hunger. Therefore, while hunger is an essential prompt, it is not enough; you also need desire. Hunger is the realization that you lack something and need it, while desire is the strong feeling of wanting it. Hunger says, 'I should read my Bible', however, desire says, 'I really want to read my Bible'. Hunger prompts your need, and desire motivates how you meet that need.

If you had only 30 minutes spare a day, what would you do with it? I imagine it would not be reading your Bible. When you are busy or tired you will choose what is easy and pleasurable. If you view reading your Bible as hard work and unsatisfying, you are unlikely to spend your precious little time and energy on it. Therefore, while you know you should read your Bible, you understandably put it off.

YOU NEED DESIRE

As discussed, God created you with innate needs to survive and thrive. Without natural food you will die physically, without real love you will die emotionally, and without spiritual food you will die spiritually. Necessity could have been sufficient, but God is good and creative, so He lovingly made provision for surviving and thriving desirable. Food can be utterly delicious, real love is immensely pleasurable and reading your Bible should be a real delight. God wants you to enjoy satisfying your needs! We are told to *"taste and see that the Lord is good"*[3] and *reading to feed* is an obvious way of tasting Him. Once you taste the goodness of God's Word, hunger will become accompanied by desire, which will increase your motivation to read your Bible.

God's Word is an essential requirement for spiritual vitality that God intends you to find utterly desirable. So why is that desire so often dampened? There are many 'desire dampers' that become stumbling

[3] Psalm 34:8

blocks to enjoying reading your Bible such as spiritual insensitivity, opposition, excuses, substitution, misconceptions, familiarity, being overwhelmed and misapplication. Let's consider these 'desire dampers' further to understand the stumbling blocks in your way.

DESIRE DAMPER ONE

Spiritual insensitivity: *"I am not hungry to read my Bible."* If you do not 'feel' hungry to read your Bible, you have lost sensitivity to your spirit's need and desire for God's Word.[4] Your spirit is crying out for its food,[5] but you are desensitized to that inner yearning. An appetite for God's Word comes from tasting and seeing how good it really is. The more you taste its goodness, the more you will want it.[6] When you do not feed on the goodness of God's Word, you lose your appetite for it. There is only one way to stimulate your appetite and that is to start feeding and to continue feeding. As you do, your appetite will awaken and grow.[7]

DESIRE DAMPER TWO

Opposition: *"I am too busy; it is not a priority."* As a Christian, you have an opposing enemy, the devil. He is very real and actively opposing your rising up in spiritual strength and empowerment. He wants you to remain spiritually weak so that you misrepresent God in this world, and miss out on the best that God has for you. The devil knows the powerful effect that reading your Bible will have in and through you. Therefore, he works to make you busy and blind to the necessity and power of reading your Bible, so that you willingly neglect it. To counteract him, take the thoughts captive that tell you, there is 'no time' and 'no point' in reading your Bible.[8] Then remind yourself why reading your Bible is essential. Then look at your busy schedule and make the time (covered in Chapter Three).

---

[4] Ps 119:25　[5] Psalm 119:131　[6] Ps 119:103　[7] Ps 119:50　[8] 2 Corinthians 10:5　[9] James 4:7

As you do, your discipline will soon be accompanied by a freshly emerging desire and renewed perspective on your Bible. God's Word will empower you with right thoughts and spiritual strength to resist the devil's oppositions.[9] Once you have experienced the life changing and reviving power of God's Word, the devil will not be able to fool you with his distractions, lies and tactics as easily.

DESIRE DAMPER THREE

Excuses: "I know I should, but…" Because you have a hunger that tells you that 'you should read your Bible', but you lack the desire, you will experience a burden to read it rather than a joy. The necessity to read your Bible should be a light and easy yoke.[10] When you carry the responsibility of studying, interpreting and applying God's Word for successful Christian living yourself, it is burdensome. However, when you rely on Jesus to allow His Spirit to teach and coach you, the burdens are lifted. After all, you make time for what you want to do and excuses for what you don't. You probably don't want to study the Scriptures every day, but I am sure you would love to sit in God's presence and learn of Him every day. Later in this book we will look at being a student of the Holy Spirit in His Word. However, for now just focus on *reading to feed* to receive and revive. Simply curl up and enjoy the nutritional and mind renewing effect that occurs (super) naturally when you read your Bible.

DESIRE DAMPER FOUR

Substitution: "I read lots of Christian books, do my daily devotional every day and attend church every Sunday; surely that's enough." The quality of your diet really matters, physically, mentally and spiritually. When you take the nutritional needs of your body seriously and put effort into eating a wholesome unprocessed diet,

---

[10] Matthew 11:30

you soon notice improvements. You will become healthier by losing excess weight, experiencing a boost in energy levels, increased mental sharpness and generally performing better as a person. It is just the same with your spiritual diet; living off books, preaching and teaching that contain Scripture is tantamount to living off processed (spiritual) food. It would have gone through another person, and come out coated by their perspectives, agendas and level of revelation. Additionally, living off small portions of Scripture in a daily devotional and a weekly sermon will give you enough to survive but not enough to thrive. Your main meals should be you reading your Bible in its entirety. Then the books, sermons and devotionals should be enhancements; 'condiments' and 'side dishes'. Why live off the additions when you can live off the main unadulterated organic, top quality food that can empower you to perform at your very best, spirit, soul and body?

DESIRE DAMPER FIVE

Misconceptions: "It's so boring and irrelevant." It is common (as I have for most of my life) to view the Bible as a book containing volumes of information that is boring and hard to read. The reality is, that when you connect with the Spirit and life that is flowing from the Word of God, it comes alive. You will begin to see God, salvation, humanity, the Church and yourself in biblical context and from God's perspective. Traditions that you have lived by will be confronted by empowering truth and your life will gain an exciting prophetic edge. You will begin reading your Bible to hear what the Holy Spirit is saying to you today, rather than just the details, accounts and events. All this replaces the perspective that reading your Bible is boring with it being exciting and thrilling, because it is life changing.

DESIRE DAMPER SIX

Familiarity: "I know the stories, so I don't enjoy reading them." Many of the major highlights in the Bible are well known, while lesser-known parts are neglected as boring, irrelevant or too challenging. It is hard to have desire for reading and re-reading stories that you know so well, or Scripture that has little natural appeal. However, when you connect with the Holy Spirit as your tutor (this is explored in Chapter Five), He will apply Scriptures to your personal circumstances and keep His Word fresh. The Word of God can be a flowing river[11] of fresh revelation that enriches you with new information from the same old favorites and less exciting parts time and time again.

DESIRE DAMPER SEVEN

Overwhelming task: "It is so big, I don't know where to start." The Bible is a big book that can be overwhelming. However, it is not a book to be read as much as it is a book to have an abiding, life-long relationship with. Start anywhere, start reading and keep reading. Read it all, believing what it says, and prayerfully seeking God in it all. The Holy Spirit will help you break down and enjoy His big book. When I first read my Bible cover to cover, I relished watching my book mark progress towards the end. When I reached the end I felt as though I had conquered its overwhelming volume and it became very accessible to me. The more time I spend in my Bible the more comfortable I feel there. You can enjoy the same relationship with your Bible and victory over its volume.

DESIRE DAMPER EIGHT

Misapplication: "I don't enjoy it; it's too much effort." The Bible is a spiritual book to be read with your spirit and for your spirit, to

---
[11] Isaiah 48:18 and Revelation 22:1

also benefit your soul and flesh. If you try to force-feed the Word of God to your flesh and soul as an intellectual exchange, you will find reading your Bible unfulfilling. However, when you read your Bible with a spiritual perspective, you will experience a connection that will lead to a growing awareness of your spiritual desire for reading your Bible. A sense of duty to read your Bible will become replaced by a sense of desire. When you are considering reading your Bible, you are not deciding whether you want to read your Bible. You are actually choosing whether you are going to follow the desire of your spirit or your flesh.

CREATING DESIRE

Your spiritual vitality is affected by your cycle of living; what you sow to you reap of.[12] What you give your time and focus to will take root and multiply in you and your life.[13] When you neglect *reading to feed*, you forget how enjoyable it is and quickly lose your appetite for it. However, when you feed, you stimulate and increase your appetite and grow to appreciate its delectable goodness.

Ultimately, you are hungry to really know God and see Him work in and through you in miraculous ways. However, to strive after that without reading your Bible is like trying to gain a degree without studying, or win an Olympic event without training. There is no alternative; you have got to diligently do and maintain the basics to enjoy the glory. God wants to do superabundantly, far over and above all that you dare ask or think, infinitely beyond your highest prayers, desires, thoughts, hopes, or dreams.[14] However, you need the miraculous work of God's Word to prepare, equip and train you. God releasing His fullness in and through you without this would be tantamount to giving a two year old a chainsaw to play with! He loves you too much to do that.

Although at this stage your main concern is bulking up with spiritual nutrition and energy, I want to look at some other benefits of

---

[12] Galatians 6:8   [13] Genesis 30:27-43   [14] Ephesians 3:20

reading your Bible to whet your appetite and stimulate your desire. The following life transforming benefits will (super)naturally occur as you read with a posture of faith to receive. Then they will be established and develop as you flow with your emerging spiritual desires.

BIBLE BENEFIT ONE

It fuels your fire. Your body is a temple[15] for you and the Holy Spirit to dwell in while on this earth,[16] and your heart is the altar within your temple.[17] You should have a constant fire of God and for God burning on your altar, burning hot rather than lukewarm.[18] The Levitical priests were instructed to never let the fire on the altar go out. They were instructed to add fuel to the fire daily.[19] For the priests the fuel was wood; for you your fuel is God's Word. Read your Bible to pile up fuel in your heart, to which God can add His fire. How ferociously aflame is your heart for God with love, passion and worship? Whatever you have, there is more. Whatever you have lost can be abundantly replenished. Through Jeremiah, God tells us that, *"He will fully satisfy the weary soul and replenish every languishing and sorrowful person".*[20] A dictionary definition of replenish is 'to make full or complete again, as by supplying what is lacking, to supply fire fresh fuel and to fill again'. If you want God to set you ablaze, simply take in the fuel of God's Word and then fan the flame with worship. The more fuel you take in and the more you fan it, the more you will feel the burn.

BIBLE BENEFIT TWO

It lights your life. The Word of God is light to flood your mind so that you can understand God and His ways in truth. It is a lamp to your feet to light your path[21] and it is the source of godly wisdom.[22] As you read your Bible consistently with an open and receptive heart, you will increasingly receive the light of wisdom

---

[15] 1 Corinthians 6:19 [16] Romans 8:9 [17] Matthew 6:21 and Hebrews 8:10 [18] Revelation 3:16
[19] Leviticus 6:12-14 [20] Jeremiah 31:25 [21] Psalm 119:105 [22] Proverbs 1:23

and revelation.[23] You will begin to evaluate things from an increasingly spiritual perspective, make decisions more akin to God's will and receive supernatural insight into your immediate and future circumstances.

It is possible for you to live at maximum effectiveness in this life. Your God ordained ascension in life is not dependent on chronological progress, it is dependent on your level of dependency on the light of God's Word to live by. Daniel, who devoted himself to God and his own spiritual wellbeing, was found to be ten times wiser than the king's diviners[24] to the extent that he could interpret the king's dream without being told the dream's contents.[25] This is not natural wisdom, this is supernatural revelation. As you nourish your spirit, you consequently nourish your spiritual faculties and therefore become more receptive to what the Holy Spirit is revealing. With a greater ability to see life from God's perspective and hear what He is saying, you will become greatly empowered in living your life effectively and supernaturally. If it is possible for Daniel under the Old Covenant, then it is possible for you under the New Covenant.

Jesus, who lived completely dependent on spiritual insight and instruction,[26] is our ultimate example of effective empowered living. Among many things, He commanded the natural elements,[27] multiplied food,[28] healed the sick,[29] raised the dead[30] and ultimately reconciled humanity to their rightful place in God.[31] Jesus was definitely operating at total maximum effectiveness. However, Jesus gave an awesome promise and challenge when He said, *"I assure you, most solemnly I tell you, if anyone steadfastly believes in Me, he will himself be able to do the things that I do; and he will do even greater things than these, because I go to the Father."*[32] Your empowerment to steadfastly believe in Jesus to do the 'greater things' comes from God's Word, from the way it illuminates and renews your mind. The more your mind is illuminated to see life from God's perspective, the more you will be empowered to confront life in God's ways.

---

[23] Ephesians 1:17 [24] Daniel 1:20 [25] Daniel 2:1-45 [26] John 5:30 [27] Mark 4:39 [28] Matthew 14:19-21 [29] Matthew 4:24 [30] Matthew 11:5 [31] Acts 4:12 [32] John 14:12

BIBLE BENEFIT THREE

It cleanses you. *"You are cleansed by the washing with water through the Word."*[33] Spiritually speaking, it is a dirty world; even your carnal self rises up and pollutes your life. Day after day you trudge through the grime of this world and it sticks. If you are not cleansed daily, all the muck builds up and your soul becomes defiled and damaged, causing spiritual dullness. The Apostle Paul puts it like this, *"Therefore, having these promises, beloved, let us cleanse ourselves from all filthiness of the flesh and spirit, perfecting holiness in the fear of God."* [34] You would feel very dirty if you missed a few days showering or bathing. What do you suppose God thinks of an unwashed spirit? David prayed, *"Create in me a clean heart, O God, and renew a right, persevering, and steadfast spirit within me."*[35] Even though David was a Worshiper of God with a heart of affection towards Him, he still recognised his need for spiritual cleansing and renewing.

BIBLE BENEFIT FOUR

It protects you from deception and makes you free. The devil works by deception,[36] to bind you up with lies so that he can steal from you.[37] Jesus works by truth to set you free.[38] However, just hearing truth is not sufficient; you must continue in the truth and it must dwell in you for you to live free.[39] When the truth is rich in you, inscribed on your heart,[40] you can recognize deception. The Word of God is active and sharp to effectively divide soul, spirit, joints, and marrow; it is a judge of the ideas and thoughts of the heart. A Christian needs to evaluate life from a biblically cleansed, spiritual perspective.[41] Your ability to accurately evaluate and divide what is of the Spirit, of the devil or of the flesh is dependent on your continually abiding in the Word of Truth. Jesus was so filled with

---

[33] Ephesians 5:26   [34] 2 Corinthians 7:1   [35] Psalm 51:10   [36] Revelation 12:9   [37] Mark 3:27
[38] John 8:32   [39] John 15:7   [40] Romans 2:15   [41] Hebrews 4:12   [42] Acts 28:27

the truth that He could hear and evaluate what He saw in a person's heart. You have the capability to be just as discerning and open to revelation for elevated Christ-like living.

BIBLE BENEFIT FIVE

It tenderizes you. Your heart is prone to becoming calloused and hard very quickly without due care and attention. Being intimate with God and hearing His voice requires a tender and pure heart.[42] There are two ways to tenderize meat: one is to pound it and the other is to marinate it (in liquid or seasoning). Would you rather keep your heart tender to God by soaking in His consecrating Word, or by constantly being beaten into shape by the circumstances of life? Tests and trials will still come, but with a heart and soul soaked in the Word of God, you will be spiritually strong to see and understand God's purpose. With a tender heart that is intimately and dependently connected to God, you can quickly respond and move forward (without grumbling),[43] to avoid unnecessary extended stays in the valleys and wildernesses.[44]

BIBLE BENEFIT SIX

It deepens your connection with God as your heavenly father. In the beginning the Word was God Himself,[45] so by taking in the Word you are putting God into yourself. The Bible is God's autobiography accompanied by His presence, so the more you read it, the more you will know God and His ways. God can seem like such a distant father, but as you abide in His Word with an open and receptive heart, you will come to know Him with an increasing depth of intimacy.[46]

[43] Numbers 11:1 [44] Numbers 14:31-33 [45] John 1:1 [46] Colossians 1:6

BIBLE BENEFIT SEVEN

It deepens your connection with Jesus as your source of life. Jesus, who is the Word made flesh,[47] said that effective fruitful living comes out of continually abiding in Him.[48] When you maintain a continual commitment to take up residence in Jesus, who is the Word of God, you will end up touching and drawing from Jesus in greater and more effective depths. The woman with the issue of blood cried from the depths of her heart, *"If I could only touch the hem of His garment I can be made whole."*[49] Then when she did, power flowed into her. As you come to the Word with a heart's desire to touch Jesus, you will make a connection with Him that will cause His power to flow into you. Occasionally visiting Jesus in His Word does not suffice. You need to establish and maintain a continual residency in Jesus who is the Word of God. You need to allow His abiding Word to continually transform you into His image.[50]

BIBLE BENEFIT EIGHT

It makes you effective for God's kingdom. You are instructed to shine brightly for Christ with a light that comes from holding firmly to the Word of Life.[51] You are also told to remain salty,[52] which comes from being salted with fire.[53] As you add the fuel of God's Word to your heart and respond to the burn, the fire will rage and evaporate all that has watered down your saltiness. Keep going with the process of adding fuel, fanning the flames and following the leading of the Holy Spirit, and you will become a bright light that God will display on a hill.[54] In time, you will become so salty that many around you will thirst for your God. Then you will advance the kingdom in ways that you cannot even imagine. You need His empowerment to shine brightly for Him. In your own efforts, you will barely manage a dull flicker. Lost people are not looking for

---

[47] John 1:14 [48] John 15:7 [49] Matthew 9:19-21 [50] 2 Corinthians 3:18 [51] Daniel 12:3, Matthew 5:16, 2 Corinthians 4:4 and Philippians 2:15 [52] Matthew 5:13 [53] Mark 9:49 [54] Matthew 5:14-15

the Church to be relevant with its well-planned activities; they are longing for the real deal.

There are so many more benefits that come from reading the Bible with a heart to receive. As you *read to feed* and experience your spirit revive within, you will experience desire rising up. Respond to that desire, and the process will simply unfold within you according to God's purposes and the level of your surrender.

MY TESTIMONY

It was spiritual hunger that drove me to read my Bible as spiritual food. I didn't turn to the Word with a particular reading plan to follow; I just wanted to feed my spirit. So I began with my hour or so in the morning, but soon I became aware that my spirit wanted more; my desire was growing. As my spirit became accustomed to my morning feed, I began experiencing hunger for the Word throughout the day. I would find myself thinking about my Bible and making time for top-up feeds. As I responded to my spiritual hunger pangs with 'on demand feeding', my capacity to consume the Word grew. At one time the thought of reading my Bible for an hour a day would have daunted me, but now I can enjoy a two hour feast and feel as though it is a mere snack. Feeding awoke me to the miracle of the Bible, and now I absolutely love my Bible and have a lifelong commitment to it. As I *read to feed,* I become more full of God yet hungrier at the same time.

For so long my heart cried out in hunger with little hope of ever being satisfied. God gives hunger to motivate, but I was demotivated. Why? Well, I didn't know that I could do anything about the hunger, so I failed to respond appropriately. God gave His Word as nourishment, but it is up to me to feed on it. I had lost my appetite for God's Word due to not feeding, but when I began to feed, I was surprised by how quickly my desire awakened.

Many years ago I read that Smith Wigglesworth, a mighty man of faith, read his Bible every fifteen minutes! I wondered how he did that, how he remembered to read it when I would barely give it a thought while caught up with the demands of each day. Now that I have experienced my spirit's desire for feeding on the Word, I understand. He didn't have to remember to read his Bible; he had a huge spiritual appetite. His spirit was so strong within him that it would call out for the Word when he needed or desired it. I imagine he felt a spiritual energy dip and then recharged by grazing on God's Word throughout the day, in the same way that we feel our physical energy dip during the day. To survive and thrive we must listen to our bodies to know what they need. We must also listen to our spirit to realize when we are spiritually low on energy and need to *read to feed* again.

As I responded to my growing spiritual desire for reading my Bible with demand feeding, other desires arose within me. My heart began to fill with a burning love for God. I began to feel my chest being pushed to capacity from the inside, as though my love for God was trying to burst out of me.

I just wanted to worship and so I did. After reading my Bible, I would worship along to gentle worship that focused on tenderness, love and intimacy. As a result, I began practicing the presence of God. It is the most wonderful thing that (super)naturally occurs from nourishing my spirit and responding to my spiritual desires as they emerge within me. I became so consumed by a desire to worship that I would long for opportunities to soak in His presence. I didn't often feel God's presence externally. I just had to release the love and passion that was building up in me. As I did, I knew in my heart that I was connecting with God, spirit to Holy Spirit on deepening levels. I began spending hours every week adding worshipping to my *reading to feed*, and the more I did the more I burned. I have become so accustomed to loving God and connecting with Him that it is an ongoing part of my life now. I continue to hide away to worship and soak, then depending on my level of spiritual vitality it spills into my day. A momentum begins and God becomes a central focus amidst my daily activities.

At the same time, God touched my prayer life. In that place of intimate fellowship, the Holy Spirit began speaking to me. He began revealing His heart to me, sharing secrets with me and placing His burdens in my heart. Suddenly I would find myself crying and praying with a heart broken for abused children and the pointlessness of the lives of people living in darkness. He then began telling me of what was happening in the hearts of others and giving me ways to speak into situations from a point of insight and revelation knowledge. My prayer life completely changed. I stopped praying about my needs and focused on filling up and responding to what arose in my heart. Often no words or only a few words are spoken, as I simply love Him with words, singing, praying in tongues and sitting quietly. The Holy Spirit began training me to be a 'Mary of secret place abiding and learning' in preparation for being a 'Mary on a mission'.

All of this (super)naturally occurred from *reading to feed*. I didn't force, contrive or create anything. The foundational basics of *reading to feed* lead to my making connections and then, as I flowed, this journey has unfolded.

Please do not compare your spiritual condition to mine or anyone else's. You must not copy anyone's spiritual burn, and you cannot spiritually revive yourself. That is the work of God's Word and His Holy Spirit. Simply do the basics and the rest will follow according to who you are in God, with a pilgrimage that is as personal to you as your fingerprints. When I started this, I was spiritually cold to reading my Bible, worshipping and praying as a lifestyle. I have now discovered a beautifully empowering truth; that the more I read, connect and flow, the hotter I burn.

ACTION STEPS

- ✦ Make and protect the time to read your Bible (Chapter Three covers this in more depth). Keep in mind that your spiritual vitality depends largely on feeding.

- ✦ Read with a receptive posture. Lay down the pressure or temptation to read independently of your tutor (the Holy Spirit). Give it time, and your capacity to hear will arise. The Holy Spirit wants to teach you how to be His student. Just sit and read and His voice will emerge (Chapter Five covers this in more depth).

- ✦ Read to taste His goodness; just look for the goodness of God in what you read. This will cause you to fall in love with God your Father, Jesus your Saviour and the Precious Holy Spirit.

- ✦ If your reading time is taken up with books, consider how you can prioritize reading your Bible. Perhaps you could fast other books for a season. It will change your life in ways that even the best Christian books cannot!

- ✦ Listen to your emerging spiritual desires and flow – give them time and expression. In this way you will be nurturing your spiritual revival.

- ✦ When you don't 'feel' like reading your Bible, acknowledge that this is the rejection of your flesh. Don't say, "I don't feel like reading my Bible." Say, "My flesh says 'no', but my spirit says 'yes'." Then choose which leading of desire you will act upon.

- Read to add the fuel to the altar of your heart, and fan the flames with worship; simply love Him. Use worship songs to help you. The more fuel, the more intensely you will burn. Giving expression to the deep cries from your spirit will take you deeper into God. Do it in secret; just you and God for a season of growth, transformation and renewal.

PRAYER

Father God, I am sorry for allowing the flames to go dull on the altar of my heart. Father, as I add the fuel, thank You that You will add Your fire. Help me to fan the flames, help me to burn for You and be salty in ways that glorify You. Amen.

PERSONAL COMMITMENT

Now I see that Your Word is essential fuel for You to set my heart ablaze and make me salty, I will commit to…

………………………………………………………………………
………………………………………………………………………
………………………………………………………………………
………………………………………………………………………
………………………………………………………………………
………………………………………………………………………
………………………………………………………………………
………………………………………………………………………

Cherished **Father God**, You are a **requirement**, a **necessity** in my life. **Help me seek You** with all of my **heart**, mind, soul and **life**.

Adapted from Deuteronomy 4:29 Amplified Bible

THREE
CARVE OUT THE TIME
TAKING TIME OUT

If you wait until you have the time, you will probably never find it, as life has a habit of filling up. So to progress spiritually, you need to look at your schedule and carve out special time for you and God. Then you will have to protect that time and adapt, to carve out new spaces in your day as your life changes.

Often what stops us is not knowing what to do in our 'time with God'. Hopefully, after reading chapters one and two you have a clearer idea of how to get started. So your cry now is probably becoming, "I want to *read to feed* but I don't have the time; I am too busy and too tired." The thought of bulk *reading to feed* and then spending time in worship and prayer could seem to be just too high a price to pay at the moment. However, if life is crowding out God, then taking time out to focus on what really matters–connecting with God and growing spiritually–is just what you need. In doing so you will connect with your destiny and live a better and more fulfilling life in the long run. So rather than thinking of *reading to feed* as yet another thing to do, think of it as taking time out to detox, heal and recalibrate yourself and your life.

Remember you are not studying, you are feasting on God's Word; His person and His presence. You are taking in its miraculous power to awaken and empower you spiritually. Rather than thinking, "I have got to study my Bible and pray," think, "I am going to curl up with the best book in the world and spend time with my favorite person; Daddy, Lord, Teacher and Lover!"

ON A QUEST

When *reading to feed* you are not reading to study about God, you are reading to seek, meet with and know Him. As when you seek Him you will find Him.[1] However, there is a clause in that agreement, and that is to seek Him *"truly with all your heart and mind and soul and life."* This is a description of such a beautiful, wholehearted exchange. Rather than placing a demand, God is expressing His desire for a deep and committed relationship. He is saying, "let's commit our whole selves to each other, you and me." Through the sacrifice and resurrection of Jesus, God has given us a way to enjoy a depth of knowing God that is as intimate as two becoming one, just like husband and wife.[2] God wants to be one with you within the boundaries of a committed relationship.

In this kind of relationship, a person seeks to win their lover's affections continually. Similarly the quest of seeking God is marked by a sense of yearning[3] and striving to be with God and live according to His ways first and foremost,[4] as a vital necessity. God called the Israelites into a covenant to seek Him and to yearn for Him with all their heart's desire and with all their soul.[5] God's desire for such a relationship still exists in His heart and is extended to all nations as expressed by Jesus, *"You shall love the Lord your God with all your heart and with all your soul and with all your mind. This is the great (most important, principal) and first commandment."*[6] The Israelites had to meet many conditions to draw near to God, but as New Testament Christians we have a better covenant[7] where we can enter in by grace.[8] However, once we accept this amazing relationship, we must co-operate with the Holy Spirit to develop and maintain it. After freely[9] accepting reconciliation with God we must strive to enter into, and remain in, His rest.[10] The more

---

[1] Deuteronomy 4:29 [2] Ephesians 5:31-33 [3] 1 Chronicles 16:11 [4] Matthew 6:33 [5] 2 Chronicles 15:12
[6] Matthew 22:36-38 [7] Hebrews 9:10 [8] Ephesians 2:8-9 [9] Romans 3:24 [10] Hebrews 4:11

time two people share together, seeking to understand each other with open and pure hearts, the more they will know, trust and rest in each other with a connection that is felt and expressed on deeper levels. It is difficult to feel this kind of passionate connection with someone you don't know very well. Reading your Bible will take you on a quest of discovery about God; who He is, what matters to Him and how He operates. As you come to know Him and sense His heartbeat, you will fall deeper in love with Him.

It is up to you to make the effort. God stretched His arms out wide on the cross ready to embrace you. He removed every barrier and obstacle to your coming to Him as a beloved child.[11] A deep intimate relationship with God is worth all the time and effort, no matter how sacrificial it may feel to your flesh. This is not works for salvation, and you are not working to earn His love. Salvation is a free gift of grace and God loves you with all of His heart. The work is you reciprocating love on Him with time, attention and affection and grace is your permission and empowerment to do so.

MAKING THE TIME

✦ ***Consider the lover:*** The wholehearted lover thinks about their love affectionately and constantly, longing to be with them as much as possible, pining and yearning when apart. They will make sacrifices to spend time in their lover's company and they will adapt their preferences akin to what their lover enjoys and prefers. This is the kind of relationship that God desires with you. It breaks His heart when, after experiencing the joy and awakening of salvation, you begin to cool down and push Him to the sidelines for seemingly more pressing things. It is all too common in marriages that after the 'honeymoon period', lovers become partners in making their lives work, rather than their relationship better. God promises that if

---

[11] Psalm 82:6

you maintain your focus on developing your relationship with Him, He will make your life work.[12]

God loves you to the point of dying for you. He is yearning to be a part of you and your life, fully and completely. He is knocking at the door of your heart saying, *"Come and dine with me."*[13] Will you cancel plans, clear your schedule and accept His invitation afresh? As you do, you will rediscover Him as your first love.[14]

✦ ***Consider the student:*** When faced with assignments, the diligent student sacrificially cuts out all distractions to study to the best of their ability. Suddenly study becomes vital, as without it they will fail or get a lower grade than they desire.

As a Christian, you are called to be a vessel of God on this earth, a vessel with purpose and assignments. What kind of vessel you are and therefore what kind of assignments God gives you is up to you. The Apostle Paul tells Timothy, *"in a great house there are not only vessels of gold and silver, but also [utensils] of wood and earthenware, and some for honorable and noble [use] and some for menial and ignoble [use]. So whoever cleanses himself… separates himself… will… be a vessel set apart and useful for honorable and noble purposes, consecrated and profitable to the Master, fit and ready for any good work."*[15] Do you want to be gold or wood? A vessel fit for the menial or for the honorable?

Set aside time to be apart from the world and with God and allow His Word to enter in to you in abundance. As you do, it will refine the gold that God has placed within you, consecrating and sanctifying you for your honorable assignments.

✦ ***Consider the athlete:*** Living for the kingdom first and foremost and keeping God first place in your life requires sacrifice, self-denial, commitment, endurance and perseverance. Time and again, people will do this for temporal rewards; medals and crowns that will fade, titles that will be taken and money that will be spent. To be the best, they will sacrifice and lay down their life in extreme measures. The

---

[12] Deuteronomy 7:9 and Matthew 6:33 [13] Revelation 3:20 [14] Revelation 2:4 [15] 2 Timothy 2:19-21

Apostle Paul states, *"Now every athlete who goes into training conducts himself temperately and restricts himself in all things. They do it to win a wreath that will soon wither, but we do it to receive a crown of eternal blessedness that cannot wither."* [16]

Your eternal crown is awaiting you at your judgment. As a Christian, you will not be judged for your sins but you will be judged for your works. The Apostle Paul exhorts Christians to watch what foundation we base our life on, revealing the eternal consequences. *"For we are fellow workmen… with and for God… The work of each [one] will become [plainly, openly] known (shown for what it is); for the day [of Christ] will disclose and declare it, because it will be revealed with fire, and the fire will test and critically appraise the character and worth of the work each person has done. If the work which, any person has built… survives [this test], he will get his reward. But if any person's work is burned up [under the test], he will suffer the loss [of it all, losing his reward], though he himself will be saved, but only as [one who has passed] through fire."* [17]

The test is the quality of your faith[18] and obedient partnership with God. Imagine your life works so far, passing through a tunnel of flames. What will survive the flames and come out the other end of the tunnel?

As I first read the Apostle Paul's exhortation, I imagined the same thing, and saw very little surviving the flames. Which was such a sobering realization. While masked behind 'good Christian living', much of what I had spent my life on was birthed and sustained in striving for earthly gain and recognition. I was living my life according to the driving and perspectives of the flesh. Therefore, most of my life works were birthed in and sustained by the flesh.

Making the time will enter you into the process of training, conducting yourself temperately and restricting yourself in all things. God's Word is written to train and equip you, and the Holy Spirit is waiting to use His Word as your coach and mentor in running and finishing your race victoriously.

---

[16] 1 Corinthians 9:24-26 [17] 1 Corinthians 3:15 [18] 1 Peter 1:7

✦ ***Consider the treasure hunter:*** A serious antique collector will pursue a precious item or discovery passionately. They will fight off competition, pay a great price to acquire it and spend their life admiring it.

Jesus describes the kingdom of Heaven as *"something precious buried in a field, for which a man will sell all he has to acquire"*.[19]

As you open your Bible, you are opening a treasure chest. God's Word is full with kingdom living nuggets of pure gold and precious pearls that will greatly enrich you, your life and the lives of many others. By taking the Word of God into yourself, you are building up your possession of the divine light of the gospel,[20] all the treasures of divine wisdom and all the riches of spiritual knowledge and enlightenment.[21]

Jesus challenges you in saying, *"where your treasure is, there will your heart be also."*[22] There is much that we can consider to be treasure in this life and make an idol of people, possessions, career and ministry. However, there is only one exceedingly precious pearl that is worth laying your life down for, and that is God, who longs to be your greatest treasure. Job said, *"If you lay gold in the dust... considering them of little worth, and make the Almighty your gold and the Lord your precious silver treasure, then you will have delight in the Almighty, and you will lift up your face to God. You will make your prayer to Him, and He will hear you."*[23]

The things that you push God to the side for are the things that you are giving your heart to and treasuring above God. By making the time to read your Bible in pursuit of knowing God, you are trading your treasure. You are laying your gold down in the dust to discover the precious treasures of God.

As you treasure His Word, you will fill up with love of and for God. You will be perfected, completed and reach spiritual maturity so that you can enjoy complete confidence in Christ.[24] How rich, confident and complete do you want to be? Make the time, open your treasure chest and seek out the gold that is laid up for you.

---

[19] Matthew 13:44-47 [20] 2 Corinthians 4:7 [21] Colossians 2:3 [22] Luke 12:34 [23] Job 22:24-27
[24] 1 John 2:5

CARVE OUT THE TIME

NO EXCUSES WILL PERSUADE JESUS

Living under grace rather than law is a great gift of God, but misunderstanding this gift can lead to 'loose Christian living'. As you read the New Testament, it is obvious that the standards for living are set higher than in the Old Testament.[25] Of the many that make Jesus their Savior, few really make Him their Lord,[26] losing their life in order to find true life in Him.[27] Christianity is about walking the narrow ways,[28] which begins with narrowing down your life to being focused on and walking towards God. It is very sacrificial, but as you do, He leads you to wide-open and abundant spaces that you could never get yourself to.[29]

You will have many excuses for holding on to your life and taking the wide pathways, telling yourself, "God understands." But God will not accept excuses, as Jesus made very clear in the Parable of the Banquet. *"And at the hour for the supper he sent his servant to say to those who had been invited, Come, for all is now ready. But they all alike began to make excuses and to beg off. The first said to him, I have bought a piece of land, and I have to go out and see it; I beg you, have me excused. And another said, I have bought five yoke of oxen, and I am going to examine and put my approval on them; I beg you, have me excused. And another said, I have married a wife, and because of this I am unable to come. So the servant came and reported these answers to his master. Then the master of the house said in wrath to his servant, Go quickly into the great streets and the small streets of the city and bring in here the poor and the disabled and the blind and the lame. And the servant returning said, Sir, what you have commanded me to do has been done, and yet there is room. Then the master said to the servant, Go out into the highways and hedges and urge and constrain them to yield and come in, so that my house may be filled. For I tell you, not one of those who were invited shall taste my supper."*[30]

---

[25] Matthew 5:20-48 [26] Acts 5:14 and Romans 10:9 [27] Matthew 10:39 [28] Matthew 7:13
[29] John 10:10 [30] Luke 14:17-24

Jesus is inviting you to sit at the banqueting table of His Word with Him;[31] will you make excuses or will you accept? I know that you are busy, so let's look at ways you can make the time.

TRADING TREASURES EQUALS FASTING

You will have to give things up to make the time, so why not make it a fast? One perspective of fasting is denying the flesh as a way of training and buffeting it,[32] to progress spiritually. Fasting and *reading to feed* is a powerful combination, so what can you fast?

- Food: Preparing and eating a meal takes time, so why not trade one meal a day for *reading to feed*.
- Sleep: You could go to sleep later or wake earlier.
- Television: Fast TV for a period of time or a length of time each day. Turn it off and start *reading to feed*.
- Reading: Change what information you are feeding yourself; trade it in for the pure nourishment of God's Word.
- Socializing and hobbies (in person or online): Just like the student with a deadline, limit your socializing and/or web surfing time to be with God and His precious Word.
- Ministering or serving in church: If you are too busy to read your Bible and minister to God because you are 'serving Him', you are out of balance and operating at a limited capacity. Your primary assignment is to love God with all that you are[33] and then serve Him from a place of devotion and dependence.

God can achieve more in one day with a 'Mary' than what could take Him years to achieve with a 'Martha'.[34] Scale back on commitments to be a Mary and in due season God will fast track

[31] Revelation 3:20 [32] 1 Corinthians 9:27 [33] Matthew 22:37-39 [34] Luke 10: 37-42

you into what He has for you. I know it is hard to lay down ministry responsibilities, and I know that people will not understand. However, in due season you will make a greater impact as a lover of God than as a servant of God.

These options may seem very extreme to you, and may make your flesh very uncomfortable, but it is just about making a choice to carve out the time. The rewards are so amazing, but you have to put the effort in; it doesn't just happen. Remember, 'when something is important, you find a way and when it's not, you find an excuse.'

As you consider making the time, reject any condemnation that is likely to come your way, and embrace this message's power to convict and encourage you into action.[35] Condemnation pulls you down, undermining your value, capabilities, worth and purposes. However, conviction calls you up higher, saying you are capable of and called to more than you realize. God loves you and He wants you to partner with Him in great and mighty things.[36]

If you are in a Christian marriage, discuss making the time with your spouse. Carve out your own time in the Word and agree ways to share your journey. Talk regularly about what you are seeing in the Word and how your relationship with God is developing. Encourage one another and share times of worship together. In this process you will go through a great transformation. Your journeys will be different, so be sensitive and ensure that competitiveness or jealousies do not creep in.

If you live in a family setting that will not support or embrace your *reading to feed* and drawing closer to God, try not to enforce your journey on your family. Simply focus on allowing God to make you salty and, in time, God will use you to make them thirsty for Himself. Allow God to work through you in His timing and ways; if you force it you will get in the way of God. He can do such marvelous things. Let Him teach you how to glorify Him in your family home in ways that are tender, loving, merciful and miraculous.

---

[35] Romans 8:1 and 2 Corinthians 7:9–11   [36] John 14:12

MY TESTIMONY

For years my husband and I had the same ongoing conversation. "We want to press into God; we know that we should read our Bibles, but we don't have any time." We were too tired to get up any earlier in the morning and too shattered in the evening. Then in February 2011, when I reached total dissatisfaction with my spiritual impotency, we decided to make the time regardless. I wanted to go at my own pace, so we agreed to separate for time with God, and then come together to share how our time went. It was hard getting up, especially as I was feeding our baby in the night. So Richard and I motivated each other, and coffee got us going! Initially, Richard would go downstairs and I sat in bed. At some point our baby would wake and I would continue reading while I fed him and he then played beside me on the bed. I felt guilty leaving my baby to play, as though I was neglecting him, but I believed it was worth the cost.

Within a few weeks my spirit began to revive, God's Word came alive to me, and my hunger and desire began to increase. Life was busy when I began this journey. I had a four month old baby, a twenty two month old toddler and a small business, but God's Word had become irresistible to me. So I responded to the growing desire and increased my reading times. I began to wake even earlier, ask my staff to watch my toddler while I cuddled my baby and read in business hours, use my children's nap times to read, sit next to my daughter to read while she watched TV and worship in the evenings with my husband. My appetite and capacity simply grew as I nurtured it with 'demand feeding'. I became so greedy as spending time with God became my obsession.

With increased spiritual insight and capacity, worshipping, praying and fellowshipping with God has become so easy and enjoyable. However, making the time remains the hardest part. I cannot express how hard it has been or the extent of sacrifice that

I have made, but it is worth it all. It is such a joy to progress with God and experience His desire to be with me. To the extent that He initiates time with me and even steps in to help me make it possible. Let me share a few of these many moments with you.

✦ *The invitation:* One night, the Holy Spirit woke me and invited me to come away with Him, but I was so tired that I sleepily said, "No." Then I felt a powerful love wash all over me, but I still said, "No" and went back to sleep. Although I felt regret, there was no condemnation, as I am on a life long journey with Him. I know that when I say "No", I have missed out on special time with God, but I also know that there are many more to enjoy. Even though I reject Him, He never leaves me or forsakes me.[37]

✦ *Help with waking early:* I used to rely on my baby to wake me early in the morning for a feed I'd to then go downstairs to read and be with God after I had re-settled him. When my baby stopped waking for feeds, I then started relying on my alarm clock or the Holy Spirit. Many times I ask God to wake me at particular times and to make me really awake to help me get up. Sure enough, many times I wake at the agreed time and often feel wide-awake.

✦ *Practical help:* I was so looking forward to 'quality time' with God. My daughter had a play date and my son was expected to have a long nap at the same time. It was all planned and I couldn't wait. However, we had a spill in the car and my home was wrecked from the weekend. So I put my son in his cot as usual and set out to quickly clean and tidy, to then enjoy time and space with God. However, five minutes after falling asleep my son was woken up. I tried to settle him by feeding him, but he would not settle. I began sobbing from being so overwhelmed by my responsibilities clashing with my desires (and probably tiredness). So I put my son back in his cot, hoping that he would settle. Then, I stood in the kitchen surrounded by mess listening to my baby wailing over the

[37] Hebrews 13:5

monitor. I fell to my knees and wanted to scream accusations at God, "I have no-one; NO FAMILY!!! I am so alone and, God, all I have is you, but you can't help me with this problem." Instead I resisted and cried, "Help me God, help me." I felt the urge to leave my baby to cry while I at least tidied my kitchen side to then go and get him from his cot. Then suddenly in an instant, as I cleaned and cried, the anguish in my heart and my baby's crying stopped. It was as though God reached in and pressed a 'pain off' button in my heart and my baby's 'sleep on' button all at the same time. My baby slept for about three hours and I enjoyed a wonderful time with God in a tidy home.

As my children grow, my life changes, and I have to constantly adapt my time with God. Consistency, adaptation and perseverance are the keys to prolonged success. I ensure I get some time in the Word each day and enjoy taking extra time when I can. On the days that I have little time in the Word or with God I reject any condemnation, but work to ensure days like that do not become a prolonged season.

I like to start my day with God to ensure that He cannot be pushed out. By doing this, I am nurturing a God consciousness in myself that carries on throughout my day. Because my sensitivity to God is developing I can experience moments of God's glory at any given and unexpected moment. Often I have such wonderful times in our study with God before the children rise. However, when they appear I have to transition, but I leave the worship on and continue worshipping as I do. One morning I had a wonderful time with God from the early hours, until the family descended on me. I transitioned rapidly from the 'throne room' to the kitchen. Then suddenly, while serving breakfast, God's presence unexpectedly consumed me. It was so intense that I thought I would die if His presence increased any more. It was only a moment, but so powerful and precious. Other times it is a much gentler start with God. I enjoy a cup of coffee in bed, and read my Bible with worship playing quietly beside me. It could be half an hour or it could be three hours. There is no prescription, only desire in such a relationship.

Occasionally I get the sense that I am wasting my life, giving all this time to reading my Bible, worshipping and praying. When I think like this, I simply remind myself that I am spending my life in the best and most profitable way. To help me counteract such accusations from my flesh or the devil, I draw on God's promises of blessings for prioritizing seeking God and His kingdom, telling myself, 'I delight myself in the Lord and He will give me the desires of my heart'[38] and 'I Seek first the kingdom and all things will be added to me.'[39] I can't lose! I am enjoying developing my relationship with God, trusting that He will bless my life.

After many months of digging in, paying the price and experiencing a serious level of stripping back, I am seeing God's blessing start to flow. My children's time spent in education is increasing, people are volunteering time to play with my son so that I can write this book (finally!) and doors are opening to this message that God has refined within me. Time is emerging that I can use to be with God without any great sacrifice and God is providing financially so that I don't have to fill my emerging time with getting a job. My prayer is for God to make it possible for me to pursue Him and His kingdom as my full time job. I long for the opportunity to spend whole days, even weeks reading my Bible, worshipping and waiting on God. Because I have proved myself faithful in fighting for the time when it has been so very hard, God is now starting to make this prayer a reality. I am thrilled to be experiencing that there is no better way for me to spend my life.

[38] Psalm 37:4 [39] Matthew 6:33

ACTION STEPS

- Look at your schedules and commitments critically.

- Choose which treasure/s you will trade.

- Protect that time, be consistent and persevere.

- Establish a discipline (20, 30, 40 or 60 minutes per day) and nurture your appetite with demand feeding, as you feel inspired.

- Protect the time; the enemy will oppose you in this, so be determined!

- Reject condemnation; tell yourself that you are on a lifelong journey so you cannot fail by missing a day or two.

- Be aware when special events are happening. For example, going away can cause problems because often your routine goes out the window. Try to plan ahead. If you don't manage to make the time to read, just resume as quickly as you can.

- Manage your own pace; push yourself while being kind to yourself. You are running your personal race.

- Be consistent. Successful bulk feeding depends on consistency as much as amount. A little less read daily is better than a yo-yo diet.

- Enjoy it and fan the experience with worship.

PRAYER

Father, I have been spending my life in exchange for so many things other than You. I have pushed You to the sidelines of my life. I am sorry. You love me and I love You. As I consider how I can carve out time for You, inspire me. Then as I begin to use that time to be with You, touch me and set my heart on fire. Amen.

COMMITMENT

Now that I know I have to 'carve out' time for reading my Bible and drawing closer to God, I will…

……………………………………………………………………………………
……………………………………………………………………………………
……………………………………………………………………………………
……………………………………………………………………………………
……………………………………………………………………………………
……………………………………………………………………………………
……………………………………………………………………………………
……………………………………………………………………………………

Loving
Father God,
I fill my heart with Your
precious Word
to live a life
pleasing
to You.

Adapted from Psalm 119:11 Amplified Bible

FOUR

READ ITS FULLNESS

EVERY WORD COUNTS

God's Word in its entirety is so rich and multi-faceted,[1] containing much more than is evident to your natural eye and comprehension.[2] Even when you can't see value in a portion of Scripture it is there, waiting to be revealed and imparted. The Apostle Paul tells Timothy that, *"Every Scripture is God-breathed (given by His inspiration) and profitable."*[3] If it is in the Bible, it is there because God inspired and breathed life into it and it has value to profit you.

While reading your Bible cover to cover (Genesis to Revelation) is not essential for *reading to feed*, it is essential for growing and maturing fully as a Christian. As you base your eternal existence on Scripture, it makes sense to continually read it all and grow[4] in your understanding of all of it.

God's Word is like a banqueting table set before you with every benefit that you could possibly desire and require. After the Apostle Paul tells Timothy that *"every word is God breathed and profitable,"* he goes on to list what it is profitable for. According to Paul's list, God's Word contains power to *"instruct, reproof, convict of sin, bring correction of error, discipline in obedience and train you in righteousness (in holy living, in conformity to God's will in thought, purpose, and action). So that you, a man or woman of God may be complete, proficient, well fitted and thoroughly equipped for every good work."*[5]

---

[1] Colossians 3:16 [2] Psalm 119:130 and 1 Corinthians 2:14 [3] 2 Timothy 3:16-17 [4] 1 Corinthians 2:6
[5] 2 Timothy 3:16-17

God's Word is to be read for its work to make you complete, proficient, well fitted and thoroughly equipped. It is written to perform a 'continuing work' within you.[6] To receive its full work and be made complete, you need to read it all. However, you also need to read it with a wholehearted dependence on the Holy Spirit, who will use it in and through you according to His purpose. Let's look at dining on the whole banqueting table and receiving its fullness in more detail.

EAT A BALANCED DIET, ENJOY A BALANCED LIFE

When confronted with such a vast banquet, it is all too easy to feel overwhelmed. You consequently stick to the limited portions of Scripture that you are familiar with and feel comfortable with. The problem with this is that you end up living on a limited, unbalanced spiritual diet and, as a result, your life tips out of balance.[7] The devil works to tempt and knock you off balance, and therefore off course, as much as he can. God's Word is your 'balancing beam' to maintain your balance to successfully walk your course.

Imagine a tightrope walker high up on the rope, putting one foot in front of the other. He has the platform at the end of the rope in his focus, but his opponent keeps throwing things at him to knock him off. The tightrope walker holds his beam in his hands, aware that how he uses his beam will be the difference between maintaining his balance or hurtling to the ground. He knows that he needs to use the entire beam skillfully to succeed. He is fully aware that if he lets go or allows it to drop to one side for too long he will fall. So he maintains a balanced hold, fixes his focus on his destination and keeps walking one foot in front of the other.

Just like the tightrope walker, you are called to walk a narrow way[8] and maintain your balance. You also have an opponent, the

---

[6] 1 Thessalonians 2:13 [7] Proverbs 3:6 [8] Matthew 7:13

devil, who is hurling ammunition at you; ammunition of lies and deception,[9] ranging from blatant violations of God's Word and vile suggestions to subtle extremes and manipulations of God's truth. His strategy is to assault your thinking with lies and temptations to knock you off balance and into his ditches of deception. The devil knows more than you or me, that the battle for your life is won or lost in your mind. So much so that he tried to use Scripture to knock and tempt Jesus off course. Thankfully Jesus was strong in the Word and able to skillfully use Scripture to maintain His balance and stay on course.[10] The devil will make suggestions to your mind that target your vulnerabilities and moments of weakness, often relentlessly. [11] Your capacity to resist and retaliate successfully depends on your spiritual vitality and level of revelation. When you are weak in spirit, you lack discernment to differentiate the voices that you hear and you lack the right responses to rebuke him with. Because it all happens in your mind, you believe that what you are hearing or battling with is your own thinking. However, there are actually three voices to discern between: yours, the Holy Spirit's and the devil's. You need God's Word in balance and context to empower you to divide and discern the voices and respond appropriately.[12] You will be able to say, "that doesn't line up with God's Word, that doesn't sound like something my Daddy would say and that is not something that my Daddy would tell me to do." When you are strong in spirit, you can wait on God and resist the devil's temptations. Reading your Bible cover to cover will increase your understanding of God's character and who you are in Christ. Therefore empowering you to recognize the enemies lies and authoritatively reject and rebuke him.[13] With God's Word used like the tightrope walker's beam, you can create a balance of spiritual strength, knowledge and discernment that will protect and lead you forward in God.

[9] John 8:44 and John 10:10 [10] Luke 4:1-14 [11] Luke 4:2 [12] Acts 28:27 [13] James 4:7

HOW CAN YOU FAIL TO USE GOD'S WORD AS A BALANCING BEAM?

You can let go of it entirely, having nothing to hold on to when the devil assails you with his lies and temptations; or you could drop it when under attack, losing your stability when you need it most; or you could hold on to one end of it so tightly that you lose your grip on the other end.

- ✦ Letting go of your beam speaks of not reading your Bible.
- ✦ Dropping your beam speaks of having a casual relationship with God's Word.
- ✦ Gripping one end too tightly speaks of focusing on elements of God's Word while neglecting other elements.

In any of these circumstances, you are vulnerable to finding yourself in ditches of deception, extremes, confusion and frustration. Without taking in the whole Word of God, you will end up living with an incomplete understanding of God and your relationship with Him. You will either live with an emphasis on the promises or the requirements. However, balanced Christian living comes when we have a firm grip on both. Lets look at this in more detail.

EMPHASIZING THE PROMISES

When you are confronted by your needs, the devil will draw you off balance by assailing you with the Scriptures that emphasize your victory and right to blessings. If you are experiencing lack of some kind, your flesh will embrace this emphasis. This will however bind you up in spending your life focusing on what you can get from God and striving to bring it to pass, rather than striving to enter His rest.

When you have this focus, your natural desires will direct you and the things or empowerment that your heart desires will become your idol. The devil knows that in this state God cannot lavish you with all that your heart desires, as He would lose you to your idols.

EMPHASIZING THE REQUIREMENTS

When you are confronted by your deficiencies, the devil will draw you off balance by assailing you with Scriptures that emphasize your need to be holy and crucify your flesh. Your flesh will take on the responsibility to achieve holiness, so that it can feel better about itself. This emphasis will bind you up in spending your life striving to be right and 'earn' God's love rather than receiving righteousness and immersing yourself in God's love. The devil knows that you will miss out on God's best, while you spend your life striving to achieve righteousness and acceptability.

The variants of these ditches are many: pursuing prosperity, recognition, success, healing, the miraculous, affirmation, acceptance to name some, but all are common to man. We are all vulnerable to ditches of some kind, but there is great hope. Pick up your balancing beam and start using it. Read your Bible cover to cover and create a new balance within yourself as you nourish your spirit, so that you progress forward with increasing stability and freedom. As you do, you will gain a perspective of God's promises and requirements in balance. Your focus will be drawn away from yourself to God, and as that happens you will transition from striving in life to resting in God with increasing confidence, assurance and peace. As you look forward to your destination of increasingly knowing God and holding God's Word closely and in balance, you will grow in your ability to walk the narrow paths with increasing resistance to the devil's assaults.

READ IT ALL, RECEIVE ITS FULL EFFECT

The Word of God is alive to actively penetrate and divide, so that what needs to be removed can be removed; and what needs to be energized can be energized. As the author of Hebrews explains, *"For the Word that God speaks is alive and full of power [making it active, operative, energizing, and effective]; it is sharper than any two-edged sword, penetrating to the dividing line of the breath of life (soul) and [the immortal] spirit, and of joints and marrow [of the deepest parts of our nature], exposing and sifting and analyzing and judging the very thoughts and purposes of the heart."* [14]

Just like a surgeon's scalpel, the Word of God can penetrate your heart and cut away the calluses[15] of pride, unbelief, fear and greed without damaging any of your faith, hope and love.[16] You are tender and sensitive to God, but life builds up calluses that harden the exterior of your heart and block full reciprocal openness with God. In order to hear, see and know God, you need a tender heart.[17] God wants an uninhibited relationship with you, and to achieve it He has made His Word sharp and penetrating to perform continual heart surgery on you. As you first start reading your Bible cover to cover, God will need to lovingly and slowly remove all the calluses that have built up over the weeks, months or years that His Word has not had the access to penetrate and divide. Then He wants to have continued access to maintain the tenderness of your heart towards Him. When your heart is hardened by a build up of calluses, you will struggle to love and worship God as He desires you to, pray as God needs you to and love and forgive as God requires you to. However, with each act of surgery, God's love will penetrate you a little deeper, and you will feel more open to Him. This kind of surgery is so precise, it leaves no scars and the immediate after effects of each removal is increasing levels of healing and freedom.

[14] Hebrews 4:12 [15] Deuteronomy 10:16, Colossians 2:11-12 [16] 1 Corinthians 13:13 [17] Matthew 5:8

An important part of this process is diagnosis, and God's Word enters in and analyzes your current condition. On the surface you may have the appearance of a godly person, but God looks on the heart, and, like a mirror, God's Word reflects your heart back to you. The truth is that many are 'good' rather than godly, and there is an important difference. Good people live to please man, but godly people live to please God. As you attentively look into God's Word, you will be shown how God sees you. Then as you take the time to examine your heart reflection, you will probably be surprised or shocked by what you see. When you measure yourself by your own standards and by comparison to others, you set your spiritual bar low. Therefore sharing many excuses for such spiritual lukewarmness with your peers. However, when you are confronted by what God says about you, your life and how you live, you realize that God sets the bar far higher. Then you begin to see that any excuses for neglecting the basics, failing to maintain your spiritual vitality and progressing forward are null and void. It is in your nature to turn away from reflections that reveal your need for heart surgery and flesh crucifixion, settling your flesh with excuses. However, to really see yourself as God sees you is the beginning of your transformation, and then sustainable ascension in life. Whenever Scripture confronts you in such a way, examine what you see and pray about it, give the Holy Spirit permission, asking Him to teach you how to submit and cooperate. Just as a cosmetic surgeon can transform a person's physical appearance, God will patiently and lovingly use His Word to transform you into your Christ-like appearance.

A full work of transformation requires the complete Word of God. Limiting your exposure to certain portions of Scripture will limit the fullness and accuracy of its work. Your flesh has a tendency to gravitate towards reading and hearing the Word of God in contexts that support its comfort zones. It is possible to read or study portions of your Bible every day for your whole life and avoid the heart surgery in all or some areas of your life, rendering you terminally incomplete. Exposing yourself to all of God's Word will leave no callous untouched. The process of measuring yourself up against God's full gospel is challenging and can be painful, but it is so extremely life giving at the same time. It is the only way to become fully at rest in God, assured of your rightful place in Him[18] and enter into the great and unimaginable things that He has for you.[19] After all, the whole point of the heart surgery is to prepare you for God's blessing and empowerment. Therefore bringing you to a place of such devotion that even if God gave you all that your heart could desire, you would remain captivated by Him, safe from being drawn into idolatry.

TAKE IT TO HEART, RECEIVE ITS LIFE

The Bible can appear completely irrelevant to your current life, until you read it as though it is personally written to you. As you read your Bible, constantly ask yourself what does what I am reading say about…

- ✦ Me?
- ✦ My life?
- ✦ The way I live?

For example, in Chapter Three, I explained to you my response to reading 1 Corinthians 3:15, which speaks of my life's works being tested by fire at my time of judgment.

Despite being a Christian for 20 years who regularly read portions of Scripture and listened to an untold number of sermons, I did not know that I would receive such a judgment. I did not realize that some will receive crowns and some will scrape through as if

---

[18] Hebrews 4:3 [19] Ephesians 3:20

escaping fire. I did not know that I had the power to choose what kind of vessel I could be for God on this earth or what kind of reward I will receive in eternity.

When reading this portion of Scripture, I realized I had missed it my whole Christian life. I had been living without this essential eternal perspective, because I did not know this Scripture and the many other Scriptures that emphasize these truths. Upon this startling discovery, I measured and examined myself and found myself falling into the 'saved, but as one just escaping through fire' category. I am so thankful that I allowed this Scripture to cut me to my heart and change my focus. I would rather evaluate and change myself now than wait until my final judgment, when it will be too late to change how I lived my life.

As you submit yourself to such a process, your perspectives will be transformed. Then your life's focus will begin transitioning from yourself to God and His kingdom. Whether you need 'healing or slaying', the Holy Spirit will use His Word to do it. Rather than limiting His effectiveness by picking and choosing which portions of Scripture will be given access to your heart, read it all, and allow the Holy Spirit to choose what He uses and how.

EAT YOUR GREENS

As discussed, it is natural to pick at the bits of Scripture that your flesh enjoys and remains unchallenged by; however, this is tantamount to living on desserts and treats. To thrive, you need to eat the whole banquet.

Imagine a plate containing a Sunday roast dinner (apologies to all the vegetarians)…

✦ *The narratives of faith adventures in God* are like the quality, tender pieces of meat. They are full of goodness and flavor, easy and enjoyable to chew.

✦ ***The detailed lists and measurements are like the bones.*** They provide structure that is vital for study and verification. If you would like to read the lists, the Holy Spirit will honour your diligence with extra goodness. However, if you would rather leave them that is also fine. Just skim read them for the marrow, like the prayer of Jabez.[20]

✦ ***The less exciting details and events are like the greens.*** They are less interesting to your flesh, but contain essential ingredients for gaining contextual understanding. Often when given a chance they can be very enjoyable, containing less obvious nourishing goodness to be discovered.

✦ ***The details and narratives are like the gristle.*** These can be repugnant to read, such as the violence, the way women were treated or the way God responded to sin in the Old Testament – but like any good autobiography God tells the story in full, warts and all. Reading the horrors of the Old Testament can give you a deep appreciation of God's grieving heart, holiness and the blessings of living under the New Covenant.

✦ ***The promises of victory and blessings are like the desserts.*** These are a delight to read, but on their own will spoil you rotten.

When enjoying the full banquet of God's Word, feel free to, cast aside the bones, spit out the gristle and enjoy your desserts, but make sure that you eat your meat and greens! When your flesh struggles to understand or cope with what you are reading, try to go beyond your comfort zone and persist with the offerings that are harder to digest. As you do, you will discover new comfort zones and greater capacities to know and enjoy God. Essentially, the Bible is a love story; a story of a loving creator coping with repeated infidelity from the object of His desires. If you read it as a love story, you will connect with God's heart throughout it all.

---

[20] 1 Chronicles 4:9-11

READ ITS FULLNESS

FULLY IMMERSE YOURSELF, GET SATURATED

God's Word is such a miraculous gift. It is where the natural and the supernatural collide. It is merely a physical book, yet at the same time it is the very essence of God and His realm. As you read your Bible, you are immersing yourself into God and His spirit and life that flows out from Himself. In Ezekiel there is an invitation to fully immerse yourself in God... *"He lead me through water that was ankle-deep, knee-deep, waist-deep and then over my head, water to swim in, water no one could possibly walk through... He told me, this water flows east, descends to the Arabah and then into the sea, the sea of stagnant waters. When it empties into those waters, the sea will become fresh. Wherever the river flows, life will flourish—great schools of fish—because the river is turning the salt sea into fresh water. Where the river flows, life abounds."* [21]

- How deeply are you immersed in the living waters that flow from God's Word to make you alive?
- Does your Bible sit on a shelf somewhere, as though you are standing on the water's edge?
- Do you read it once a week as though you are going in ankle deep?
- Do you read daily devotionals as though going in knee deep?
- Do you read a chapter or page a day as though going in waist deep?
- Are you pursuing and nurturing a relationship with your Bible as though going in over your head, fully immersed?

You can dive in, get saturated and experience the life of God penetrating your whole being. Immersing yourself in God's Word will revive your stagnant waters with His abundant life, so why hold back?

[21] Ezekiel 47:3-10

MY TESTIMONY

I began my journey through my Bible again because I was frustrated by the lack of power in my life. I started reading my Bible saying to God, "Give me Your power", but He said, "Give me your heart", so I did. I credit the degree of my awakening and transformation to the fact that I read my Bible cover to cover with an open and repentant heart. The things that I read continually impacted me and because I opened my heart and responded humbly, God's Word was enabled to transform me steadily and progressively.

When I read my Bible cover to cover in 1996 the Holy Spirit focused predominantly on healing. As I read through my Bible I was introduced to the God that I did not know. As I came to know Him intimately, to bask in His presence, He miraculously fixed my broken heart so that I could function as a whole person once again. When I started reading my Bible, I was suicidal, dehumanized and without hope. It was a miracle the way God used His Word and presence to reach in and transform my pitiful state to one of hope and purpose. I am convinced that no person, in a lifetime, trained or untrained, could have completed the work that took place in my heart that year. If I had not read my Bible cover to cover, I would have been divorced, propelled into further distress and possibly dead or institutionalized. I had been beaten repeatedly as a child and by the age of 13 was sleeping on the streets and abusing substances. I then lived in children's homes, where I suffered further abuse. Over the years, I endured physical abuse, emotional abuse, neglect, sexual assault and rape. I was broken, broken and broken. God's Word is sharp, but the Holy Spirit uses it so tenderly when required. If you are broken, take the time to immerse yourself in God's Word and presence fully, and as you do you will be immersing yourself into His loving, careful and skillful healing hands, which in time will make you whole.

Then in 2011, when I began a similar journey, I was in a different place, I was stronger and full of pride. This time, reading my Bible cover to cover introduced me to the God that I had forgotten and neglected. Time and time again I was cut by how much I was neglecting God and treating Him with insolence. This surprised me, as I was considered to be one of the most on fire women of faith amongst my peers. However, the Holy Spirit saw into my heart and confronted me with my incessant infidelity, idolatry, laziness, carnality, selfishness, impatience, independence and greed. With His Word, the Holy Spirit showed me that I didn't love Jesus, not really, and that I was living a Christless Christianity. I was living my life saying, "Stay at the sidelines Jesus, I am busy trying to make my life work." The Holy Spirit took me through the refining fire, and the amazing thing was that it didn't hurt. Not much anyway, instead it was a beautiful life giving process. As I read my Bible cover to cover, I saw the emphasis on seeking first God and I became convinced that it is the only way to live. I was so enlivened by the process of sanctification that I became hungry for fresh convictions. I wanted more because with every cut that I submitted myself to, I was falling more in love with God and His amazing, miraculous Word. As I write this, I feel tears welling up in me, as it was such a special time. I have found my sanctification just as miraculous as my healing. I am amazed at how the Holy Spirit can cut you apart ruthlessly without causing pain. I was full of remorse and repentance but, without a drop of condemnation, I love conviction and I live for it. Although much work has taken place, I am far from complete. The work continues to varying degrees within the changing seasons of my life. I never want to stop receiving convicting reflections from God's Word and the Holy Spirit's surgical work.

Reading cover to cover made these processes possible, because they gave me the whole picture, with not a word left out (apart from the lists). With a contextual perspective of God's Word, the devil loses his influence to use Scriptures for condemning me when I am broken, or sustaining my pride when I am puffed up, and so I am increasingly free. The Scriptures that 'cut me' are wrapped up in His love and acceptance and the Scriptures that tell me 'I can have it all and do it all' are wrapped up in His requirements. Now that I read my Bible cover to cover, I can see much more of life in biblical and spiritual context. In 1996, God's Word lifted me out of ditches of depression, and in 2011, God's Word lifted me out of ditches of independence. Both ditches were destroying my life but God's Word has restored my life and continues to do so. Thank You, Daddy!

The depth and magnitude of my awakening, restoration and transformation did not come solely from reading my Bible cover to cover. Reading my Bible ushers me into the presence of God and gives me the capacity to abide there. It is reading God's Word to be in God's presence that results in such a miraculous personal revival, healing and transformation. There is a saying, "All the Word and you dry up, and all the spirit and you blow up." My journey is one of the Word awakening and enlivening my spirit, so that I can connect with God, spirit to Holy Spirit and submit myself to His work within me, continually.

ACTION STEPS

+ Read it all; remember the plate of food.

+ Don't take responsibility for memorizing it. Put it into yourself and trust the Holy Spirit to write it on your heart and bring it to your memory as required.

- Confront what you see; look at it and accept it. This process will transform you layer by layer.

- Read the Old Testament with a New Testament perspective…
  When you read *temple* – read *you*,
  When you read *priest* – read *Jesus/you*,
  When you read *high priest* – read *Jesus/you*,
  When you read *enemy* – read the *devil*.

- Persevere; nothing of great worth comes without perseverance. Your flesh will want to give up or skip parts and the devil will want you to give up, but keep going.

- Be patient; trust the process and don't give up, even if the process does not meet your expectations.

- If you struggle with reading the Old Testament, persevere to tap into the immeasurable riches of God's Word. In the next chapter I will teach you how to look to the Holy Spirit, who can bring it all to life.

- Enjoy where you are at; try to avoid racing through where you are, looking forward to the next book or the New Testament. Absorb yourself where you are. I received life-changing revelations from Leviticus and Deuteronomy.

- Read expectant to receive something. Don't ask God to speak to you; He is speaking to you all the time. Ask Him to open your ears and eyes to receive what He is saying to you each day.

PRAYER

Father, I need a full work in my heart. I am sorry for neglecting aspects of Your Word. Help me to embrace Your Word in full and help me to connect with it, and receive its full work within me. Amen.

COMMITMENT

Now that I know that I need to read the whole Bible to live a balanced life and be made complete, I commit to...

....
....
....
....
....
....
....
....

READ ITS FULLNESS

Precious **Holy Spirit,** I honour You as my Comforter, **Counselor, Helper,** Intercessor, Advocate, **Strengthener,** Standby and **Teacher** of all things.

Adapted from John 14:26 Amplified Bible

FIVE
YOUR ULTIMATE LIFE COACH
YOU HAVE THE AUTHOR OF LIFE WITH YOU

The Bible was written by various human scribes, who wrote under the direction and inspiration of the Holy Spirit.[1] The Holy Spirit is the author of your Bible, and as the author, He knows His Word inside out and to its uttermost depths. He knows how to accurately and precisely use it to transform you and your life with maximum effect.

When you read your Bible, the Holy Spirit hovers over it, longing to breathe life[2] into what you are reading. He is yearning to open up the full treasures of His Word[3] to anyone that will listen to Him.[4] His role is to be your teacher and empowering life coach; to teach you all things and bring to your remembrance God's Word, as you need it.[5] God gave you every advantage in knowing and living His will for your life. He inspired its writing and breathed His life into it. Then sent Himself in the person of the Holy Spirit to be with you, to coach you in understanding and living it. When you open up your Bible, He is right there with you.

Imagine yourself sitting reading your Bible, and as you read, you say to yourself, 'I don't understand this, I am not getting anything from it, this offends me, I will study books and manuals to gain understanding.' Now imagine the Holy Spirit sitting next to you saying, 'I know what you need to hear from what you are reading in this season or moment, let Me explain it to you, if you could see

---

[1] Revelation 1:1-3 and Romans 16:25 [2] Genesis 1:1-3 [3] Proverbs 2:4 [4] Psalm 25:14 [5] John 14:26

this the way I see it, you would see its beauty or power.' The Holy Spirit looks at you lovingly and sorrowfully as you rely on your own abilities, rather than His tutorship.

The problem is not grappling intellectually to understand or using additional study materials; the issue is what, or who you are leaning on? Are you leaning on the flesh, or are you leaning on the Holy Spirit?[6] The flesh will interpret what you read in the light of the past, present and limited biased perspectives. The Holy Spirit will interpret what you read in the light of all eternity, and complete knowledge of your heart, circumstances and God's ways. It is when you connect the author of God's Word with your life that reading your Bible becomes life giving, prophetic and exciting!

CONNECTING WITH THE ULTIMATE TUTOR AND LIFE COACH

It is mind blowing to think of the Holy Spirit, who is God, hovering near to you yearning to be your personal tutor. He is so big and awesome and you are so small; how could it be? The prospect of connecting with the Holy Spirit as your personal coach and tutor may seem unrealistic or impossible. However, it is the reason that He came and it is easier than you may think. The author of Hebrews sets out four faith and action steps that lead to a very powerful connection. We looked at them in Chapter One, but let's look at them again.[7]

✦ ***Step one—Salvation:*** You need to accept Jesus as your only way to the Father.[8] Jesus lived on Earth to carry the sin of the world to the cross. He was slain as the final sacrificial lamb on behalf of all humanity,[9] and then resurrected[10] to overcome the power of sin and death, once and for all.[11] He did this so that you can be regenerated in spirit and cleansed by His blood to stand blameless before a Holy God.[12] By simply acknowledging and receiving this gift, you will be

---

[6] Galatians 3:3 [7] Hebrews 6:4-8 JB Phillips [8] John 14:6 [9] Isaiah 53:1-6 [10] Matthew 28:6 [11] Romans 5:10 [12] Acts 15:11

rescued from darkness and transferred into the light[13] of God's love for eternity. Then, as His adopted heir, you gain access to all that God is and all that He has for you.[14]

✦ *Step two—Receive the Holy Spirit:* Before Jesus' death, resurrection and ascension, the Holy Spirit came upon[15] people for specific empowerment. After these miraculous events, the Holy Spirit now lives in people[16] for daily-empowered living. By simply being invited in, the Holy Spirit will enter in to begin refining and empowering you as His temple. For worship, prayer, holy living and displaying His glory.

✦ *Step three—Knowing the wholesome nourishment of the Word of God:* You need the nourishment of God's Word to be alive spiritually so that your spirit can rise up above your flesh, connect with the Holy Spirit and lead you in living.[17] Walking in unity with the Holy Spirit will lead you into the great and mighty things that He has prepared for you.

✦ *Step four—Touch the spiritual resources of the eternal world:* The more spiritually alive and sensitive you become, the more you will connect with, and draw upon, the spiritual resources of the eternal world. Your growing connection will cause you to live with the increasing perspective that God's eternal world is more real than your temporal world. Therefore living increasingly for God's kingdom,[18] compelled and empowered to partner with God in transforming this world.

Each of these steps require action:

✦ Praying a prayer to receive salvation.

✦ Praying a prayer to ask the Holy Spirit into your heart.

[13] Colossians 1:13   [14] Romans 8:17   [15] Judges 3:10   [16] 1 John 3:24   [17] Ephesians 6:10   [18] Matthew 6:33

- Carving out the time to *read to feed*.
- Looking for and nurturing the connection.
- Flowing with what you receive.

They also require faith:
- Believing that you receive salvation.
- Believing that you have received the infilling of the Holy Spirit.
- Believing that you are receiving nutrition from God's Word.
- Believing that you can connect.
- Believing that the Holy Spirit is speaking to you.[19]
- Believing what you hear in your spirit.

You can't force this connection; it will simply happen as your reviving spirit rises up within you to lead you in making the connection. Then the more you flow with it, the more you will receive and progress.[20]

HOW TO MAKE THE CONNECTION

Once again, imagine yourself sitting reading your Bible, with the Holy Spirit sitting right next to you. Now imagine yourself engaging Him in what you are reading. You might struggle with this concept saying, "But I can't hear God" or "I don't know when He is speaking to me" or "I can't feel His presence". You are not alone in this; connecting with the Holy Spirit to receive from Him with clarity and precision is probably one of the greatest desires and frustrations of most Christians. God wants you to know His voice so that He can communicate with you clearly and precisely. You heard His call to salvation and you responded, so you can hear Him. You simply need to develop your spiritual vitality, and therefore ability and sensitivity.

[19] Mark 11:24 [20] John 15:4

To flourish in sensitivity, discernment, courage, stability and accuracy, you need the Holy Spirit and the Word of God in unison. The Bible is the written Word of God, and the Holy Spirit speaks the Word of God. He inscribes it on your heart and brings it up to your surface as you need it. Your responsibility is to put the written Word in and expectantly rely on God to work with it, within you by His abiding Holy Spirit. In doing this, you are acting in faith; by giving space and time to connect and, consequently, grow. Let's look at 'putting the Word in' and 'the work of the Holy Spirit with the Word in you' in more detail.

PUTTING THE WORD OF GOD IN

We looked at this in great detail in Chapter One. As you read with a faith perspective that God's Word is nutrition for your spirit, your spirit will begin to revive within you. Without spiritual nutrition, your spirit lies weak within you, while your flesh remains strong to connect with the world on a flesh-to-flesh level and drown out the spiritual. In this condition your five physical senses are 'in charge', constantly telling you how to live. However, as your spirit becomes revived from its nutritional surge, your spiritual senses become awakened and your spirit has emerging strength to assert itself over your flesh. Just like tipping the balance on a set of scales. For a season you have been tipped in the balance of your flesh, however, as you *read to feed,* you begin tipping the balance in favor of your spirit. As a child of God, you are made with spiritual senses that, like your natural senses, require nourishment and use to be effective. Simply 'put the Word in' and trust that the reviving effects will take place. As you do, your ability to *hear*[21] the voice of the Holy Spirit, *see*[22] with spiritual insight, *feel*[23] the presence of the Holy Spirit, *taste*[24] the goodness of God and perhaps even *smell*[25] the spiritual realm will emerge with increasing sensitivity. You will begin to read your Bible with your spiritual senses

---

[21] John 10:27 [22] Ephesians 1:18 [23] Psalm 51:11 [24] Psalm 34:8 [25] 2 Corinthians 2:15-17

and connect with the Holy Spirit as your tutor. He will take you on an exciting personalized tuition course, life development program and pilgrimage to the heart of the Father God.

You cannot force this process, no matter how much you wish, pray, practice or step out in faith. You cannot rise up in spiritual strength and touch the spiritual resources of the eternal world in accurate, progressive and mature ways without feeding on the nourishment of God's Word. This is good news because if it was a matter of how clever or spiritual you are, it would be a biased process. Thankfully, you have as much chance as any other child of God to connect with the Holy Spirit and receive all that He has to tell, show and give you, because you are made for it.

THE WORK OF THE HOLY SPIRIT WITH THE WORD IN YOU

The work of the Word is a work of transformation.[26] To purify your heart, refine the gold that God has placed within you and teach you how to live for Him. This work is based on revelation and it is the Holy Spirit who is the revealer of all things. When you read your Bible, begin by including Him in your time. Do not ask the Holy Spirit to speak to you; He is always speaking to you. He is zealously reaching out to you with a yearning heart and passionate jealousy. Make a faith connection by thanking the Holy Spirit for being with you as your tutor and coach, asking Him to help you to receive. Pray for wisdom, discernment, opening up of your ears, eyes and heart, but don't ask Him to speak. As your spiritual senses revive, you will connect and begin to receive in a number of ways.

✦ ***Drawing:*** You will experience your spirit's desire grow for spiritual things, but part of this is actually your growing awareness of the Holy Spirit drawing on you to be with Him. We talk a lot

---

[26] 1 Thessalonians 2:13

about wanting the Holy Spirit's presence, but He wants you. He wants your attention so that your mutual relationship can grow deeper and so that He can teach you how to live your new life. As you respond to the sense of wanting to be with God, you are responding to the Holy Spirit's call to be with Him. The more you say yes to Him, the more you will recognize His call and develop in your capacity to be in His presence.

✦ *Highlighting:* As you read your Bible, the Holy Spirit is poised to speak. He will start bringing things to the surface from what you are reading to gain your attention. It can either surface suddenly, as though a verse or word jumps out at you, or it can surface very subtly, in a way that is easily missed. However, just like playing *'Where's Wally?'*, once you have experienced it a few times, it will become more obvious to you. It can be a sense that there is more to come from what you are reading, like the Holy Spirit is tapping on your heart saying, "Stop a moment, I want to explain something to you from this." Or, it could be like hearing an echo of what you are reading, as though the Holy Spirit has already begun talking to you, expecting you to stop and listen. When this happens, you need to stop and give it your attention. So that like Samuel you can say, "I am listening!" At first it might just be a little thought, but as you give it your attention it will grow within you. The best way to capture the unfolding revelation is to start writing the initial thought down. Then as you do, additional thoughts may flow and what you are hearing will grow or consolidate on paper. Keep writing until the flow stops, then review what you have written and pray about it, if necessary. It doesn't have to be anything big; it could be just a few words or it could be paragraphs. The Holy Spirit works line-by-line, precept-by-precept. You may not realize it, but with each line you are being transformed. If when you stop reading to listen nothing flows, don't be concerned; just continue reading and trust the process.

✦ ***Themes:*** As you read through your Bible, you will notice themes, as though they were being pointed out to you. From a number of verses over a short or long period of time you will see the same theme arising, and sense that it has significance. The Holy Spirit may also draw on your surroundings to accentuate what He wants to speak to you about. This could be from a conversation, daily devotional, road sign, sermon or email to name a few. As the theme arises, give it your attention and work with it. As you do, you will gain clarity and understanding.

✦ ***Dialogue:*** As you read your Bible, ask questions about everything and anything; even personal and relational issues. Perhaps about a situation that you face, what you are feeling, or for further clarity on a decision you have to make and so on. If you ask the question, you will recognize the answer when it comes. Be bold in this; ask and expect an answer, then actively look for it from what you read. Whatever surfaces, write it down and give it time before acting, unless the Holy Spirit tells you to act sooner.

✦ ***Interpretation:*** The Holy Spirit will use His Word to speak into something that you are experiencing or have experienced in the past. Perhaps a hurt, a sin, clarity on an event or even a dream that you have had. Quite simply, as you are reading, your thoughts will suddenly be drawn to what the Holy Spirit wants to deal with and at the same time the Scripture will speak directly into it. As you stop and give this your attention, the Holy Spirit will work on your heart and mind, giving you new perspectives or prophetic insight. Write it all down and give it time to grow within you.

✦ ***Weaving:*** As you read your Bible, the Holy Spirit will put Scriptures together to bring clarity and greater insight. It is as though He is saying, "Remember when I said that in the other verse? Well that is what I meant in this verse." These are wonderful moments of illumination given as a gift to fast track your growth, often as preparation for something ahead.

✦ ***A bolt of lightning:*** This simply comes out of nowhere. You just suddenly see something that you didn't see before. This is the Holy Spirit lifting a veil and shining a light on something new that He wants you to see. The revelation may come while reading or at another time.

✦ ***Droplets:*** Thoughts enter your mind, suddenly and seemingly out of nowhere. Although it is an internal thought which seems to be your own, its entrance and content seems out of context of your current thoughts and activities. This can be the Holy Spirit or demonic suggestion. The richness of the Word of God within you, your growing spiritual vitality, spiritual connection and maturity will empower you to divide and discern, as discussed in Chapter Four.

✦ ***Knowing in your knower:*** When asked, "How can I know when God is speaking to me?" Christians often reply, "You just know in your knower." Well, what is your 'knower'? It is your 'gut instinct' or your 'sense of peace', which can be a good general guide. However, on its own, how you feel is too unreliable and vague to base your life on. Emotions change, agendas influence, your flesh conflicts with your spirit and the devil works to confuse and tempt you. God created you to have clarity of thought and purpose. So He gave you His Word, and the ability to hear Him clearly and specifically. As you flood yourself with God's Word, your mind will be renewed, your sensitivity to God's voice will develop and your 'knower' will become a discerning spirit. It is this combination that empowers you to live with godly clarity and purpose.

✦ ***Visions:*** Your spiritual sight can be so developed that you can see into God's eternal realm. You will either be shown in the eyes of your spirit or taken out of your body on 'a tour', so to speak. I have never experienced this, but it happens and it is biblical, so it is possible. Personally, I think I would love it, although it might overwhelm me.

✦ ***Dreams:*** God speaks in dreams and when He does, He can use His Word to confirm, clarify and interpret. One night I dreamed that I was attacked by a man with a cricket bat. It was in a park at night and I was pulled down on to my knees. Then I woke up and I found myself reading so much about attack and violence. God used His Word to confirm that it would happen and that I must pray. Two days later, a family member endured an almost identical attack, but serious injury and death were averted.

✦ ***An audible voice:*** Almost every time I have heard the Holy Spirit, it has been with an internal voice, that feels and sounds like my own thoughts. However, I have heard His voice audibly at least once. In 1996, in my year of intense healing, I was home alone, sitting in my lounge silent before God, when He simply said, "Kim, I love you." It was so real, that I responded and said, "I love you too", before realizing that it was an unusual experience!

✦ ***Prophecy:*** God is a prophet, who brings things to pass by speaking into the future.[27] His Word is a lamp to your feet and a lamp to shine along your pathway so that you can see where He wants to take you.[28] As you connect spirit to Holy Spirit, He will start prophesying to you and through you. You don't have to be a prophet to hear God or speak prophetically and it is far more natural than 'thus sayeth the Lord'. Using any of the ways above, He will simply speak to you prophetically. You may not realize it is prophetic until the Holy Spirit pulls things together.

✦ ***Renewing of your mind:***[29] This is the most important aspect of your tuition, as without a renewed mind you will remain immature and unstable. Everything, absolutely everything, about your life is affected by how you think. As you read your Bible, the Holy Spirit will use His Word to change the way you think. His aim is to use His Word to cause you to evaluate life from a spiritual perspective over and above a natural perspective, to become more like Daddy.

[27] Romans 4:17 [28] Psalm 119:105 [29] Romans 12:2

WRITE IT ALL DOWN

Every Word that the Holy Spirit speaks to you is precious, so you must write as much as you can down, no matter how small. I like to use 'Post-it' notes, as it is interactive with my Bible. As something surfaces, I lean on my Bible, start writing on the note and then stick it in my Bible alongside the relevant Scripture. If it is a little note, I write in the margins. My first Bible in this pilgrimage doubled in thickness due to the many 'Post-it' notes and they are all so precious to me. They are a record of my personal conversations with the Holy Spirit with His precious Word. They contain what He has said, my response and gestures of affection, such as kisses and smiley faces. Reading your Bible should be a totally interactive and relational experience. Without this, everything else that I have written becomes a ritual that soon dries up. If I had not written down every word, including even the smallest surfacing word, my pilgrimage would have lacked the same impact. I would have missed so much of what the Holy Spirit was saying to me. By writing it all down I caught it, allowed it to grow and now I retain it as a record and treasure. Find a method that works for you best – 'Post-it' notes, a journal or an electronic device to name a few. Listen for even the smallest hint of something rising up. As you start to write it down, much of it will grow into something very special and personal.

GIVE IT TIME

After you have written a note, read it back and pray about it, then write your responses down to follow on from your note. It can be so simple; perhaps you read about resting in God's arms[30] and it impacts you, thinking, "I want that", so you write, "Daddy, I want to rest in your arms; teach me how to climb up and stay there." He will love that. All of this increases the focus that you give to the

---

[30] Deuteronomy 33:27

Holy Spirit. It is a structure for drawing near to Him, because He first drew near to you. It is the 'faith act' of giving Him this time and focus that will enrich the whole experience and strengthen your connection to then go on and receive.

As I have said, with every communication, insight and note, the Holy Spirit is transforming you line-by-line, precept-by-precept. Committing to the Holy Spirit as your tutor and life coach requires patience and laying down your flesh. It is so easy to turn to a textbook, search engine or person, but if you delay such instincts, you will give the Holy Spirit time and develop your reliance upon Him. Read and keep reading your Bible, depending on the Holy Spirit. Flow with what surfaces and leave your questions with Him. In our information rich world, we are used to accessing things instantly, but connecting with the Holy Spirit requires 'being still' to know and receive.[31] Having access to information and people to speak into your life is a great enhancement, but lean on the Holy Spirit and let Him lead you to enhancements as you need them. The answers and revelations will not always come instantly or while you are reading your Bible; they can come at any unexpected moment. When you nurture a vitally active spirit to Holy Spirit connection, you, in a sense, live in 'receptive mode'. A mode of daily consciousness of the Holy Spirit and ongoing biblical meditation upon the abundance of God's Word within you. Then at any moment, because of your vitally active connection, answers and revelation will come. It could be while you are reading your Bible or worshipping or even having a conversation with a friend. The Holy Spirit will simply reveal something new and you will be enriched. It is much more fun this way, as the answers come in dynamic and life-giving ways. Give Him the chance and He will really show off His tuition and coaching skills to you. Remember, the whole point of *reading to feed* is not for information, it is to draw nearer to God in intimacy and transformation. When you choose to read your Bible to touch the

---

[31] Psalm 46:10

very depths of God's heart, you will begin to yearn daily for a fresh connection with the precious Holy Spirit and become determined to get to know God with increasing intimacy. Then intellectual knowledge and comprehension beyond your own reasoning will be given as a gift. As I have written, your spiritual growth is not chronological like physical growth, it is determined by the depth of your connection, reception and response; the more you surrender your flesh, the more you will grow in spirit.

Just like in the film 'The Karate Kid', the Holy Spirit is like Daniel's coach, Mr. Miyagi, who agreed to train Daniel in Martial Arts. Daniel was a complete novice and anticipated learning how to fight. However, Mr. Miyagi had Daniel painting fences and waxing decking! Daniel became so frustrated, thinking that the training was a waste of time. But Mr. Miyagi knew what he was doing and after time, but in an instant, Daniel realized that he had progressed much further than he thought. If you dare to resist running here and there and slow down, in the natural realm you will have a sense of loss or wasting your time and missing opportunities. In time, however, you will realize that you have gained so much more. The Holy Spirit can bring it all together and fast track you at any moment, so be patient. It will include trial and error, but keep your connection with the Holy Spirit strong and He will bear you up and keep you going, coaching you along the way.

MY TESTIMONY

Anyone, absolutely anyone, can enter into this process and be transformed according to God's ways and purpose. I began this process in 2011 as a complete novice in living the way that I have written about. I had little capacity or appetite for giving myself to reading my Bible, praying, worshipping and building an intimate relationship with God. The power of my testimony is that if I can do it, anyone can. No person has taught me what I share with you in this book; it is the fruit of leaning on the Holy Spirit and flowing with Him.

You can connect with and receive from the Holy Spirit without reading your Bible. I connected and received many times over the years of my Christianity, experiencing accurate words of knowledge and miraculous answers to prayer. However, regularity, clarity, purpose and progression were missing and God felt so distant from me. I was groping in the dark and remaining largely unchanged. Since *reading to feed,* I have experienced increasing clarity and intimacy that is unquestionably attributed to reading my Bible in the way that I have shared with you in this book. It is connecting with the Holy Spirit as my Tutor and Coach on a regular basis that has brought my Bible alive. Without Him, it would still be so dry to me. I was, without question, a 'lukewarm' Christian with a hardened heart. I began reading my Bible saying to God, "Give me your power" and He said, "Give me your heart." And I did; I laid my heart open and accepted every Word that He said, embracing every conviction with a repentant and open heart. I never tried to excuse myself and I sought the Holy Spirit's empowerment to change, and I still do. I found the growing intimacy and tenderizing of my heart so life giving. I was surprised to find myself in the refining fire and sense no pain. However, at the same time, the Holy Spirit started to turn the heat up to target deeper issues. While the circumcising of my heart (that I describe in Chapter Four) was such a beautiful experience, the circumstances that the Holy Spirit took me through at the same time were very painful. I find the Holy Spirit's 'School of Intimacy' to be Heaven on Earth, but His 'School of Faith' at times feels like Hell on Earth!

The circumstances that my spiritual revival began in were circumstances of isolation, loneliness, financial lack and grief. After enjoying a short successful season in business, I quickly lost everything that I had gained, including selling my home to pay off debts. All I had strived for was gone.

By the beginning of my spiritual revival I had my long awaited miracle baby girl and then my baby boy, a small lifestyle business and a spacious rented home. However, we were scraping by financially and I had moved away from the community that I had lived in for 20 years. As a result, I was restricted financially, lonely and exhausted. I had no family to help (particularly no mother) and I was feeling let down by my church 'family'. In all this, my business was a vital lifeline for me. It was a soft play facility that I ran as a business and ministry of my church. It provided me with an income that fitted my role as a mother, but it also gave me an identity, purpose and somewhere to go. Some of my staff would even cuddle and watch my children, so that I could escape and read my Bible. In my intensive program of refining, God targeted three areas. My reliance upon people, my reliance upon money and reliance upon myself.

RELIANCE UPON PEOPLE

Being suddenly so isolated and lonely, I began grieving not having parents. I don't know my father, and my mother had little capacity to be a mother to me. At the point of moving house, I lost the little contact that I had with my mother and moved away from my friends. With my babies, lack of company, lack of support and little financial reserve, each day had become about survival. My husband had a good job, but it resulted in my having to do it alone much of the time. There was no one to visit or help me, and no one for me to call on or go out with. My heart broke at the thought that there was 'no one on this whole planet that loved me enough to visit and help me at their own personal expense, as a loving mother would'. In the first year, two people came into my life promising to be like family to me, but it didn't work out. One was too busy and the other friendship went sour. As I shared my journey and message, many were inspired and encouraged; however, my closest friend and church leaders that I had walked with for years became my critics. I was called a radical, told to seek professional help, told to give up developing this book in favor of getting more involved in my church and to leave such 'basic Bible reading' in favor of more advanced forms of Bible study. All this caused great pain and I began to question my value and likability and the devil used all of this to tell me that I was 'no good'. I experienced hurt, anger and rejection many times.

I was mourning a community I knew and loved, I was mourning having local friends, I was mourning my own home, I was mourning prosperity and finally I was mourning being part of a church. The only thing that kept me attending my church was the fact that my business was an integral ministry. I feared that leaving my church would mean having to give up my business, so I kept going, all the while praying for release.

This refining was intense and painful, but I kept reading my Bible and listening to the Holy Spirit and as I did, I saw God at work. God was teaching me how to love people, but rely on Him for all of my needs, including my emotional needs. He was moving my dependency on flesh to dependency on Him.

RELIANCE ON MONEY

I have spent years striving to make money. I wanted to be financially independent, living in my own spacious family home and able to hire domestic help when my babies finally arrived. Although I had made great gain in this area, I lost it all around the time that my baby girl came into the world. The subsequent opening and success of my little soft play business was a miracle and absolute blessing that God made the way for. However, I started to believe that I could not manage financially without the business. The income was seasonal and when I first saw the income dip, I started to panic. Then the Holy Spirit told me that I was making an idol of my business by looking to it as my provider. In the first year He showed me that we could manage on a smaller income, then in the second year He invited me to give my business away and go on a faith adventure with Him! He told me that life would be radically different on the other side of giving my business away. It was not a command but an invitation, and one that we could decline without any condemnation. My husband's salary would just cover our rent and utilities but there was nothing left over for food, other basics or any luxuries. My husband and I talked and prayed and then accepted the Holy Spirit's invitation and handed our business over to another couple in our church. Since then, we have been learning how to live by faith financially, even for food. While I do not enjoy living so financially restricted, I do enjoy seeing the ways that God provides and our growing capacity to trust God as our provider. The cost of this decision was high to me. I gave away my income, ministry and identity within my church and community. The Bible says that God loves a joyful giver, but when I wrote the email confirming that I was transferring my business, I was crying my heart out, although I knew I had heard from God and did not want to hold back.

RELIANCE UPON MYSELF

I was independent with a capital 'I', and when I initially experienced blessing in my business and career I became so full of pride. God was trying to strip me back for years and I was inviting it. However, each time it came to the crunch and things looked hard or impossible, I found my own way out, creating my own solutions. At the beginning of my Christian life I tried 'living by faith' but didn't see the results I wanted in the time frame that I thought I needed to. So I made an internal decision to sort things out myself. As a result, I embarked on a life of double-minded Christianity. I had one foot in the camp of faith and one foot in the camp of do-it-yourself, and I was struggling in both. I had a sense of what God could do with my life and I desperately wanted Him to do it, but I took over, trying to bring it all to pass myself. I knew that I needed to seek God first and that He would then add to my life. However, I felt as though I didn't have time to simply 'seek' Him, as my needs felt too pressing and urgent. In being stripped back, I laid down striving and ambition, gave up looking to people to promote me, and developed my trust in God. It has been the best thing I could have done. I am learning to lay down my flesh and wait on God, for His best in my life.

It has been tough, but I am thankful for it all. I would have experienced many of the tough circumstances with or without holding God's hand, but by holding His hand I have been guided through it all with eternal and spiritual perspectives. While it has been a time of painful and costly pruning, it has also been a time of intensive fertilizing. A season that is proving to be one of my most fruitful to date. He has taken me through valleys that lead to new mountaintops. I know without question that God has stripped me back to bring me to points in my life where I only have hope in Him, and this time I have not resisted or run away. I have laid it all down and said, "Crucify my flesh according to your purpose and ways."

As I (and my husband) have surrendered to the stripping back and refining, we are now experiencing God's rebuilding of our lives. We have endured many tests and, since *reading to feed,* we have begun passing the tests. From our new kingdom perspectives we have proved that we are prepared to go the distance with God and resist creating our own ways in life.

We are having old friendships strengthened, and new godly friends added. God is connecting us with church leaders who have a like spirit and heart after God's presence. He is opening doors to this message that I carry in my heart and has joined Richard and me with seasoned ministers to birth a church that prioritizes God's presence. I now have friends volunteering to provide childcare so that I can write this book that I thought I may never finish. All this is the fruit of my hiding away and going on the pilgrimage that I have been sharing with you in this book, and I know this is just the beginning; God is truly amazing!

By surrendering to the intense flames, I have been refined and will continue to be. God has skimmed off much scum and purified some of the gold that He has placed within me. The teaching and testimony of this book and my developed faith in God is such precious gold that I value immensely.

ACTION STEPS

+ Engage the Holy Spirit; treat Him as your tutor and expect Him to teach you.

+ Interact with your Bible; ask questions and write down as much as you can.

+ Give yourself and the process time. Resist any time restrictions on receiving answers or bearing fruit, unless the Holy Spirit has given you specific time frames.

+ Commit to the Holy Spirit as your primary teacher; look to Him for the tuition.

+ Maintain a repentant and open heart and resist putting up excuses.

+ Hide away with God as much as you can, don't seek to promote yourself out of the growth you experience; God will place people to call the gold out of you when it is ready.

- Resist the 'Pharisee' (hypocrite) within. As you grow spiritually, your flesh will begin to judge others; resist this at all costs as it will kill your progress.

- Lay down your flesh to die as much as you can.

- Seek two or three confirming words from the Holy Spirit – through your Bible, people and surroundings before stepping out on a Word. If you are not sure, wait.

PRAYER

Holy Spirit, I am sorry for dishonoring You by treating You as though You are not with me. I am sorry for relying on the flesh, rather than You. Help me to turn to You and teach me how to depend on You more and more. Give me the patience and courage to wait on You when running to the flesh would be easier. Amen.

COMMITMENT

To connect with the Holy Spirit as my life coach and tutor, I will…

....
....
....
....
....
....
....

YOUR ULTIMATE LIFE COACH

Glorious
Holy Spirit,
I am your temple,
You are living in me.
I am not my own,
help me to bring **honor**
and *glory* to You
in my body.

Adapted from 1 Corinthians 6:19-20 Amplified Bible

SIX

THE FLESH

YOUR FLESH IS A PRECIOUS GIFT

I have mentioned the flesh quite a few times so far, with an emphasis on nurturing your spirit and mastering your flesh. This emphasis is not to say that your flesh is 'bad', but rather a precious gift from God that needs good management. Your flesh enables you to connect with and enjoy the entities of this vast and rich natural realm. It is your temporary tent and temple, given to serve the real eternal you while you live on this earth. Let's look at this further.

A TENT

The Apostle Paul refers to the body as a temporary tent: *"For while we are still in this tent… not that we want to put off the body (the clothing of the spirit)."* [1] The Apostle Peter also refers to his body as a tent: *"I think it right, as long as I am in this tabernacle (tent, body)… Since I know that the laying aside of this body of mine will come speedily, as our Lord Jesus Christ made clear to me."* [2]

Your body is a covering that blesses you with physical substance and senses to connect with, experience and enjoy the physical realm.

A TEMPLE

The Apostle Paul states, *"Do you not know that your body is the temple (the very sanctuary) of the Holy Spirit who lives within you."* [3] While your body is your tent to live in, it is also a temple for you to worship

---

[1] 2 Corinthians 5:4 [2] 2 Peter 1:13-14 [3] 1 Corinthians 6:19

God in, and for the Holy Spirit to fill with His presence.[4] He desires to live in you to share life with you and empower you to live beyond your physical restrictions, so that He can reach out through you.

Your body is given to be a blessing, without which you could not operate in and experience this world. You need it to enjoy a hug, hold hands with a loved one and feel the warmth of the sun. God planned life on Earth to be filled with blessings and joy, and He gave you a body of flesh to maximise your enjoyment. It is important that you love, enjoy, cherish and care for your body, as stated by the Apostle Paul, *"For no man ever hated his own flesh, but nourishes and carefully protects and cherishes it, as Christ does the church."*[5] However, the Apostle Paul also teaches that you must master your body: *"For this is the will of God... that each one of you should know how to possess (control, manage) his own body in consecration (purity, separated from things profane) and honor."*[6]

The first step in this mastery is having a right perspective of your flesh. It is too easy to live as though you are your flesh; but as we have seen, you are spirit and soul and your flesh is a gift to serve your spirit and soul temporarily. When you live as though you begin and end in your flesh, you will lack the perspective required to master your flesh. Therefore, you will allow your flesh to rule you, run your life and 'ground you' to the natural realm. However, viewing your flesh as 'yours' rather than 'you' will begin to set you free from its dominance. Then you can take off to soar above and beyond your natural restrictions and enjoy new levels of freedom in supernatural living.

WHAT IS THE PROBLEM WITH YOUR FLESH?

As discussed, your body of flesh is a blessing that needs to be mastered (controlled and managed). When it is not mastered, it becomes an encumbrance that holds you back from your full, God ordained potential. However, your flesh is not your problem, but rather your

---

[4] Acts 2:4 [5] Ephesians 5:29 [6] 1 Thessalonians 4:4

management of it is. Just as a good parent loves and trains a willful or disobedient child, you need to love and train your flesh.[7] If you do not, your flesh will lead you away from God and His best for your life. This is because your flesh is in opposition to God and His ways;[8] your flesh has a tendency to be weak, selfish, limited, unreliable and corruptible. Let's look at this in more detail.

THE FLESH IS WEAK

Jesus said, *"The spirit indeed is willing, but the flesh is weak."*[9] Your flesh is strong in living for itself, but it is weak in living for God, His kingdom and truly for others. Your flesh simply does not have the strength, capacity or empowerment for spiritual things. It may seem like a good idea to your flesh to read your Bible, fast, pray, worship and so on, but your flesh will run out of staying power and give up. This is because your flesh struggles to understand or enjoy the benefit of spiritual activities and will resist giving time to them. For example, your spirit loves to 'be still and know God',[10] but your flesh feels as though such passive inactivity is a foolish waste of time. Your flesh will get bored, distracted or frustrated and want to 'DO SOMETHING!'

However, while your flesh is weak, be encouraged and empowered in the knowledge that your spirit is willing and as you nourish your spirit, you will add strength to its willingness. Jesus said it this way, *"True (genuine) worshipers will worship the Father in spirit and in truth."*[11] It is really hard to be a true worshiper in the strength of your flesh, but it gets increasingly easier and enjoyable in the strength of a willing, nourished and strong spirit.

[7] Galatians 5:24 [8] Galatians 5:17 [9] Mark 14:38 [10] Psalm 46:10 [11] John 4:23

THE FLESH IS SELFISH

Jesus taught that you should live a selfless life: *"love your enemies and be kind and do good [doing favors so that someone derives benefit from them] and lend, expecting and hoping for nothing in return."*[12] He also lived the ultimate example in this: *"Just as the Son of Man came not to be waited on but to serve, and to give His life as a ransom for many [the price paid to set them free]."*[13] Jesus surrendered to that cross for you with no guarantee that you would receive His gift and live out its empowerment.

Supernatural living is laying down your life for others while placing upon them no expectations for anything in return. As a child of God, you can be confident of who you are in Christ and live for others as a service to God, who will abundantly reward you.[14] Unfortunately, because your flesh cannot live with this eternal perspective, it will struggle to live in such a way, and will regularly revert to 'self' mode. As you try to live a selfless life of love and service, your flesh will end up being overwhelmed by the personal cost, inconvenience and impact. It will begin to resent any lack of recognition or reward and lead you into regret, despair, 'victim mode' and, ultimately, resentment, thus wiping out your love investment.

Your spirit knows how to love and serve others, by looking to God for direction and purpose to serve supernaturally, as unto God.[15] The more you connect with the Holy Spirit, the more He will share His heart for others with you; serving can become an exciting joint venture. You can live life as though you are a secret blessing agent of God, who, as your 'employer', will provide you with all the resources that you need and reward you handsomely.[16] What an exciting thought!

---

[12] Luke 6:35 [13] Matthew 20:28 [14] Matthew 6:3 [15] Colossians 3:23 and Ephesians 6:7 [16] Colossians 3:24

THE FLESH

THE FLESH IS LIMITED

As previously discussed, your flesh is limited to your experience of the natural realm as defined by what your body can touch, see, hear, smell and taste. However, there is so much more to life than this. All physical matter began with the Holy Spirit, who spoke it into existence. So as the Spirit created the natural, which is temporal, we can conclude that the spiritual realm, which is eternal, is more real than the natural realm. Because your physical senses struggle to connect with the spiritual realm, you are lead to minimize its reality in your thinking and living, therefore limiting your interaction with all that it has to offer. The problem with this is that when you experience pain, infection or injury, you accept sickness, although, *"By His wounds you have been healed."* [17] When you experience lack, you accept poverty, although, *"God will liberally supply (fill to the full) your every need according to His riches in glory in Christ Jesus."* [18] When you experience depression, confusion, fear, rejection, loneliness or anxiety you accept despair, although, *"God will guard him and keep him in perfect and constant peace whose mind [both its inclination and its character] is stayed on You, because he commits himself to You, leans on You, and hopes confidently in You."* [19] As you journey through your life, your flesh will limit your options in your own situations and in the situations of others. However, your spirit will connect you with the inexhaustible resources of God's supernatural realm. It won't all fall into place straight away. As you commit to nourishing your spirit and fellowshipping with the Holy Spirit, you will go from faith to faith, glory to glory and strength to strength, in breaking free of the physical limitations.

[17] 1 Peter 2:24 [18] Philippians 4:19 [19] Isaiah 26:3

THE FLESH IS UNRELIABLE

Living the Christian life successfully requires stability in thought and reliance upon God. When we waver, we are tossed about by the elements, which threaten our success. James explains it this way, *"Only it must be in faith that he asks with no wavering (no hesitating, no doubting). For the one who wavers (hesitates, doubts) is like the billowing surge out at sea that is blown hither and thither and tossed by the wind."*[20] As a Christian, you are called to walk on water, mastering and overcoming the waves as you go,[21] rather than be tossed about by them. When the waves threaten the flesh, it panics and runs around looking for the nearest and easiest retreat, screaming, 'it's impossible, prayer doesn't work, God doesn't hear me, God has left me'. If you live life believing your flesh, you may never reach the destinations that God has for you, as your flesh will talk you out of it when the going gets tough. Empowerment to navigate the storms successfully comes when you flood yourself with God's Word and walk forward hand-in-hand with the Holy Spirit with a reliance upon Him to get you to the other side. However, it can be nail-biting living this way and your flesh will often struggle because the Holy Spirit will lead you straight into the winds. When confronted by the tempests of the waters that you have dared to step out onto, you need a stable focus to keep going. While your flesh will forget all that it knows about God in such moments, your spirit will draw on the Holy Spirit for direction, encouragement and assistance to know and take the next steps.

Walking out into the impossible usually begins with the Holy Spirit giving you compelling insights into what is possible with Him. Losing sight of what He has shown you will cause you to lose sight of your destination. Stability and reaching your faith destinations come from fixing your gaze on Jesus, His promises and believing that He will not fail you and bring it to pass. Only your spirit has the capacity to do that when the storm is raging all around you. Then

---

[20] James 1:6 [21] Matthew 14:29

when you come through the other side, your flesh will 'catch up' and what once threatened your flesh begins to seem like a mere breeze.

THE FLESH IS CORRUPTIBLE

My dictionary describes the word corruptible as 'a willingness to act dishonestly for personal gain' and as 'in a state of decay'. Your flesh is unavoidably ageing towards eventual physical decay, but what about its tendency to live for personal (temporal) gratification and gain? Is this unavoidable too? The answer is no, not if you are a born-again Christian. At the point of salvation your flesh was redeemed,[22] bought by the precious blood of Jesus.[23] It now belongs to Jesus and He expects it to be used for His glory, and what He expects, He makes possible. With spirit to Holy Spirit empowerment and good management, your flesh can be used to glorify God in increasing measure.[24] This empowerment comes by recognizing your flesh's continual vulnerability to corruption so that you can begin to take charge. There is no condemnation in recognizing the true limitations and rebellion of your flesh, as it is not the real you. Its nature is common to all humanity, through all the ages as expressed by the Apostle Paul, *"But [now] I am fearful, lest that even as the serpent beguiled Eve by his cunning, so your minds may be corrupted and seduced from wholehearted and sincere and pure devotion to Christ."*[25]

Recognizing your flesh's constant vulnerability to corruption is very empowering, as it positions you to deal with it. The devil wants to draw you away from God and His best for you, by tempting your flesh at its vulnerable hotspots. God told Cain, *"Sin is crouching at the door, eager to control you. But you must subdue it and be its master."*[26] God is saying the same thing to you and me. The Apostle Paul gives some insight on how to do this, *"Strip yourselves of your former nature [put off and discard your old unrenewed self] which characterized your previous manner of life and becomes corrupt."*[27] As you read the verses

---

[22] Galatians 3:13 [23] Ephesians 2:13 [24] 1 Corinthians 7:23 [25] 2 Corinthians 11:3 [26] Genesis 4:7 NLT
[27] Ephesians 4:22

around this verse, the reality of your struggle and your empowerment become clearer. To live this verse, you need to renew your thinking, which will, in turn, empower you to stop doing the things that you should no longer be doing, with a flesh that belongs to Christ.

Remember, *reading to feed* is taking in…

- The nutrition from the Word of God that renews your mind, so that you increasingly think like God and embrace His supernatural perspectives.
- The energy from the Word of God that causes a vibrant passion for God and His ways to flourish within you.

Reading to feed, while flowing with your increasing spiritual capacity and obeying what you receive in your spirit, is your pathway to mastering your flesh and soaring supernaturally.

YOU MUST DIE TO TRULY LIVE

This may seem like an alarming statement, but let's explore it further, as it is actually radically empowering and liberating. Jesus set the precedent for us by laying down His life to open up free access to God's presence and eternal life. If Jesus did not die on the cross on your behalf and rise in victory over the power of death, then you would not be able to be reconciled to God by grace. Your only way would be to satisfy the entire law.[28] I don't know about you, but that would definitely count me out.

So before we even start looking at this further, the principle of death leading to greater life is already established by Jesus, who endured death to make a way for all to receive eternal life.[29] Thank you, Jesus!

[28] Hebrews 10:1-3 [29] Hebrews 12:2

THE FLESH

That includes you; God gave His very best and His absolute all for you, and He asks you to make the same sacrifice in return. Jesus tells us that, *"He came that they may have and enjoy life, and have it in abundance (to the full, till it overflows)."* [30] However, He also explains, *"whoever is bent on saving his [temporal] life [his comfort and security here] shall lose it [eternal life]; and whoever loses his life [his comfort and security here] for My sake shall find it [life everlasting]."* [31] You have to lose your temporal (natural, flesh) life to truly live your supernatural, eternally empowered life! As highlighted by the Apostle Paul, *"And those who belong to Christ Jesus (the Messiah) have crucified the flesh (the godless human nature) with its passions and appetites and desires."* [32] This is as costly as it sounds, but it is worth it because the rewards far outweigh the costs. So how do you lose your life to enjoy your abundant Christ won life? Well, it comes through continually building up your spirit, submitting to sanctification and walking it out… let's look at this further.

BUILDING UP YOUR SPIRIT

We'll go back to the beginning of this book. Whichever is stronger, your spirit or flesh will lead you in living. It is futile trying to master/crucify your flesh with a strong flesh and weak spirit. Your flesh wants supremacy and therefore fights for it. Trying to battle your flesh in the strength of your flesh will bring you down. Think about the following statements… *"Any kingdom that is divided against itself is being brought to desolation and laid waste"* and *"no city or house divided against itself will last or continue to stand."* [33] In essence, trying to master/crucify your flesh with the strength of your flesh is like trying to persuade your flesh to commit suicide! However, build up your spirit and you will increase and develop your ability to master/crucify your flesh in the strength of your spirit.

[30] John 10:10 [31] Matthew 16:25 [32] Galatians 5:24 [33] Matthew 12:25

Whatever you are struggling with, this is your answer for continued and consistent victory over your flesh.

Wherever your flesh is stronger, you are vulnerable to sin. Whatever your issues may be: laziness, greed, anger, gossiping, addiction or fear to name a few – they are the lusts of your flesh. The devil presses your areas of weakness with suggestions and temptations, trying to get you to compromise and sin. If you try to resist the suggestions and temptations in the strength of your flesh, you will most probably be feeding the issue with your focus and attention, and therefore prolonging your struggle. However, turn your focus to feeding your spirit and submitting to the Holy Spirit (as taught and testified in the previous chapters) and you will be empowered to suffocate the very life out of the issue. Your strong spirit will empower you to say 'no' and your renewed mind will find the suggestions and temptations less and less appealing, in favor of God's alternatives, according to the desires of your spirit.

SUBMITTING TO SANCTIFICATION

God wants you to host His presence powerfully, but to cope with and maintain that you need to be humbled under the mighty hand of God.[34] Before you can be supernaturally empowered and promoted beyond your hopes and prayers, you need to be stripped back; in essence, you decreasing, so that God can increase.[35] To achieve this, God will purposely narrow down your options and prune unwanted growth to draw you more fully to Himself and His ways in devotion, dependence and trust. Let's look at this further.

NARROWING

Jesus invites you to 'enter in' to all that awaits you in Him, *"Enter through the narrow gate; for wide is the gate and spacious and broad*

---

[34] 1 Peter 5:6 [35] John 3:30

is the way that leads away to destruction, and many are those who are entering through it. But the gate is narrow (contracted by pressure) and the way is straightened and compressed that leads away to life, and few are those who find it." [36]

Imagine yourself standing in front of a gate. You can't see much of what is on the other side, but what you see looks good. You receive an invitation to go through and you are tempted, but it looks too narrow for you to fit through. You realize that you have to leave aspects of who you are and what you have behind to fit through, and you start counting the cost. At the same time, you see another path, which is wide, unhindered and you can take it without personal sacrifice. To your flesh, the wide path will seem to be the best option, but is it? Jesus had the same choice to make. When in the wilderness, the devil tempted Jesus with power and authority in exchange for His worship, but Jesus declined.[37] He had already seen the possibilities laid out for Him behind the narrow gate of physical and spiritual death. The devil offered Jesus easy access to a counterfeit promise, which had He accepted, He would have received just a shadow of what God had promised Him. In the same way, your life is filled with similar choices…

✦ The wide gate of living off preaching OR the narrow gate of reading your Bible for yourself.

✦ The wide gate of carving out your own career/ministry OR the narrow gate of hiding away with God and allowing Him to work in you until He deems you fit for promotion.

✦ The wide gate of holding on to the little that you have OR the narrow gate of gaining so much more as a result of giving up what He asks you to.

✦ The wide gate of giving in to your flesh OR the narrow gate of denying your flesh and flowing with your spirit and the Holy Spirit.

[36] Matthew 7:13-14   [37] Luke 4:4-8

The flesh looks for the easy self-ingratiating ways forward in life, while the spirit waits upon and obeys the Lord, even if it feels like death to self. Every gate leading to new and abundant places in God will require you to lay things down in order to fit through. As you look at your gate wondering why you can't enter in, it may be that the Holy Spirit is asking you to put something down and trust Him that what is on the other side is far better.

I have laid many things down to progress with God, even praying, serving and tithing. Under the convicting tuition of the Holy Spirit, I soon saw that I had been going through the motions of following the ways of flesh and tradition for years. In response, I laid down praying so that the Holy Spirit could teach me how to pray and allow Him to pray through me; I laid down serving so that the Holy Spirit could prepare me for more effective and powerful service; I laid down tithing to learn New Testament Holy Spirit and love-led giving. My life and time is too precious to spend on things that are birthed in, and sustained by my flesh. I am learning to hide away with God and sit at His feet in worship and adoration, knowing that He will put what He has placed and developed in me on display (in due season).

Ultimately, God wants total trust and dependence. He wants to strip away all else that you lean on, so that He can prove Himself faithful to you 'time and time again'; beyond what you can currently imagine or believe.

PRUNING

God created you to be a beautiful garden that He can enjoy and cultivate as a blessing to many others. As expressed by Solomon, *"I am my beloved's [garden] and my beloved is mine! He feeds among the lilies [which grow there]."*[38] The Apostle Paul says, *"For we are fellow workmen (joint promoters, laborers together) with and for God; you are God's garden and vineyard and field under cultivation."*[39]

---

[38] Song of Solomon 6:3

Imagine yourself as a garden that has many untended areas and God looking beyond your current overgrowth at your hidden potential. He knows that there is so much more for you to be and to enjoy. In the areas of your life that your flesh is not stripped back, your life will be stifled with weeds and briars that cover and suffocate your true beauty and potential. God longs to be your landscaper, to lovingly cultivate you. Initially, the cultivation will require pruning, which can be costly, challenging and even painful. However, as the overgrowth is removed, you will experience greater space to enjoy God and your life. Then the pruning will be maintained by the Holy Spirit, who will watch for any negative regrowth to 'nip it in the bud'. As quoted by the Apostle John, *"He cleanses and repeatedly prunes every branch that continues to bear fruit, to make it bear more and richer and more excellent fruit."*[40] This work is a beautiful cooperation between the Holy Spirit and you. The more you flow and trust, the less painful the process will be; with each phase being completed closer to God's intended time frame.

As a garden, your loving landscaper wants you to be…

- ✦ Pruned back – things designated by God cut away, laid down or given away.
- ✦ Fertilized – nourished by the Word of God.
- ✦ Watered – satiated by the Holy Spirit.
- ✦ Deepening your roots – become increasingly established through fellowship with God and like spirited Christians.
- ✦ Bearing fruit – more abundant, rich and excellent fruit, through abiding in the Word and obedient living.
- ✦ Establishing growth – be maintained and pruned in new areas.

[39] 1 Corinthians 3:9   [40] John 15:2

WALKING IT OUT

Walking it out is how you establish any new work of God's Word and the Holy Spirit in your life, long term. The Christian life can be full of wonderful moments of revelations, healing and deliverance, only to be lost in the face of challenges and testing of your newfound freedom and victory. After receiving fresh revelation, healing or deliverance, you must establish it in your heart and life. You must be a doer of the Word, as well as a hearer,[41] to maintain freedom gained and a stable walk.

From a young age I struggled with anger, and in the early days of my marriage, my temper flares became very ugly and regular. I would swear the worst words that I could think of to get my husband to understand how much 'he had hurt me'. The anger would build up in me to the point of causing me physical pain, if I did not let it out. Then finally, in a church conference I experienced deliverance. Although there was no way to test my new freedom, I knew that something had broken off my life and I was elated. Then to my surprise, the very next day I faced the same pressure to rage in anger just as before experiencing deliverance, as though nothing had changed. As the anger grew and threatened to burst out of me, I realized that I had two choices; give in at the first test, or walk out and establish my new freedom. So I resisted the feelings by behaving opposite to how I felt, while meditating on just two relevant Scriptures.

"Refrain from anger and turn from wrath; do not fret—it leads only to evil."[42] I knew the evil outcomes of giving in to anger and I didn't want evil in my life or family.

"So be subject to God. Resist the devil [stand firm against him], and he will flee from you."[43] I continually resisted the devil's temptations to give in to anger with a full expectation that he would leave in this area of my life. Although it took about three weeks of resisting the anger, I have been free ever since.

[41] James 1:22 [42] Psalm 37:8 NIV [43] James 4:7

Because I walked out my deliverance, I established a new freedom in my life. However, had I submitted to the temptations following my deliverance, I believe my victory would have been lost. In fact Jesus warns, *"But when the unclean spirit has gone out of a man, it roams through dry [arid] places in search of rest, but it does not find any. Then it says, I will go back to my house from which I came out. And when it arrives, it finds the place unoccupied, swept, put in order, and decorated. Then it goes and brings with it seven other spirits more wicked than itself, and they go in and make their home there. And the last condition of that man becomes worse than the first."*[44]

As you walk it out, you will be tested. The devil will challenge your resolve and God will test your faithfulness and readiness. Going to new levels involves…

✦ Preparation – feeding and sanctifying.

✦ Testing – walking it out.

✦ Qualifying – proving your faithfulness in your new area of development or freedom.

✦ Promotion – new blessings and responsibilities.

All of this takes time; often far longer than you would like! Unfortunately, it is the issue of time that usually breaks resolve and faithfulness. As time passes and you are 'still' experiencing the pruning, narrowing and testing, it is very easy to become discouraged and give up. However, if you maintain your feeding and fellowship with the Holy Spirit, you will begin experiencing the right eternal perspectives and spiritual empowerment to pass the tests.

The Israelites were led from Egypt (the land of just enough), to go through the wilderness (the land of not enough) to enter their land flowing with milk and honey (the land of more than enough). We expect to progress in life chronologically. However, God in His absolute wisdom takes us through a thorough process of testing to

---

[44] Matthew 12:43-45

qualify us for far greater blessings and responsibilities. How you walk through the tests will dictate how quickly and victoriously you enter into whatever abundance God has promised you. The Israelites took 40 years to complete a journey that could have been completed in weeks. What kept them there? Their continually failing the tests due to natural and temporal perspectives dominated by the lusts of their flesh. They grumbled against God and failed to trust Him, despite appearances. The New Testament puts it this way, *"For we walk by faith [we regulate our lives and conduct ourselves by our conviction or belief respecting man's relationship to God and divine things, with trust and holy fervor; thus we walk] not by sight or appearance."*[45]

YOUR FLESH WILL SABOTAGE YOUR BLESSING

As you regularly feed your spirit, submit to sanctification and walk it out, your flesh will do one of two things: resist what God wants to do or hijack what God is doing. Your flesh will unwittingly keep you out of your 'promised land', either afraid to step out or unable to enter in. Let me explain.

✦ *The resistance of your flesh:* Your flesh will struggle to fully believe God or cooperate with Him. My flesh resisted reading my Bible for years, telling me that reading my Bible regularly was unnecessary and irrelevant. It enjoyed all the preaching, focusing on the 'word of faith' and prosperity Scriptures, but didn't want the discipline of reading my Bible cover to cover. Since committing to *reading to feed,* I still experience the resistance of my flesh. Although now that I have tasted and enjoyed the goodness of God's Word, my flesh can never talk me out of regular *reading to feed.*

✦ *The hijacking of your flesh:* As you begin to experience continued victory and breakthrough from *reading to feed,* your flesh will become excited by what is happening and take the credit. Without

---

[45] 2 Corinthians 5:7

THE FLESH

you realizing it, your flesh will become puffed up with pride and get carried away with your newfound spiritual revelations, experiences and growth. Your flesh will become impressed with how much you love God, read your Bible, pray or worship and look down on those who don't. It will begin to glory in and take credit for what 'it' has done and should therefore share with others, 'all for the glory of God'. To make matters worse, some people will start paying you compliments, which the devil will feed into; telling you how well you are doing and what you should be doing next. Then before you know it, you are floating around on a 'super spiritual cloud' dreaming about who you are (and can be) in God.

As I *read to feed* and become immersed in loving God, I experience my flesh rising up to hijack my spiritual progress continually. My only hope is to look to the Holy Spirit to help me master my flesh DAILY, all the while resisting any condemnation. When I am tempted to think too highly of myself, the Holy Spirit gently says, *"Beware the Pharisee within."* Knowing what Jesus thinks of the Pharisees,[46] this sentence has a powerful circumcising effect on my flesh. When I begin thinking I am something special, I recognize it as the prideful tendencies of my flesh and seek to make every imagination that exalts itself against God within me obedient to Christ.[47]

There is absolutely nothing wrong with dreaming big in God, but when God births dreams of greatness in you, He is simply inviting you into a process of training and preparation. A taste of greatness does not make you great; it simply tests your readiness. Consider Moses, who stepped out as a deliverer of the Israelites to end up in the wilderness;[48] or Joseph, who announced His calling to be a great leader,[49] to end up a slave.[50] Both became great men of God, but when they thought they were ready, God knew that they were not. The saints in the throne room of God cast down their crowns to worship God.[51] A person who continually casts down every great thought and victory at the feet of God to worship

[46] Matthew 3:7 and Matthew 23:27 [47] 2 Corinthians 10:5 [48] Exodus 2:13-15 [49] Genesis 37:6-10 [50] Genesis 37:28 [51] Revelation 4:10

Him, is a person fit for greatness. Resisting even the smallest hint of pride as though it were your greatest enemy is essential for going all the way with God.[52]

HOW TO COOPERATE WITH GOD'S LANDSCAPING

Narrowing and pruning can be painful and costly, and it is natural to resist and shrink back, quoting, *"Therefore, [there is] now no condemnation (no adjudging guilty of wrong) for those who are in Christ Jesus."* However, this promise applies to those who also *"live [and] walk not after the dictates of the flesh, but after the dictates of the Spirit."*[53] Walking after the dictates of the Spirit will free you from following the dictates of the flesh, which open you up to condemnation. In every area that you allow the Holy Spirit to prune and maintain you, you will be free from the accusations of the devil and your own flesh. In these areas of your life you will be able to say, like Jesus, *"The prince (evil genius, ruler) of the world… has no claim on Me. [He has nothing in common with Me; there is nothing in Me that belongs to him, and he has no power over Me.]"*[54]

As a child of God, condemnation does not belong to you and God will never narrow or prune you with condemnation. He will, however, discipline you as a loving Father. Your challenge is to submit to this aspect of His fatherly love for you, as expressed by the author of Hebrews, *"You must submit to and endure [correction] for discipline; God is dealing with you as with sons. For what son is there whom his father does not [thus] train and correct and discipline? Now if you are exempt from correction and left without discipline in which all [of God's children] share, then you are illegitimate offspring and not true sons [at all]."*[55]

Condemnation is from the father of lies, who will pull you down. Condemnation points out your failures and limitations resulting in feelings of hopelessness, defeat and shame. When you experience

---

[52] Proverbs 16:18 [53] Romans 8:1 [54] John 14:30 [55] Hebrews 12:8-9

this, resist the lies, but ask the Holy Spirit if there is anything in you that the devil is using to bring the condemnation.

Conviction is from the Father of Life, who will raise you up (in due season). Conviction also points out your failures and limitations, but at the same time tells you that you can be so much more and do so much more (in Him); resulting in feelings of hope, aspiration and dependence. When you experience this, wholeheartedly accept what He is telling you, make no excuses and repent. Then walk it out in the knowledge that you are a loved child of God preparing for entering into greater things.

PASSING THE TESTS

Many delayed blessings and empowerments are caused by failing to pass tests. God has many promotions planned for you, but He cannot take you to the next level until you have passed the current tests. As stated by Peter, *"So that [the genuineness] of your faith may be tested, [your faith] which is infinitely more precious than the perishable gold which is tested and purified by fire. [This proving of your faith is intended] to redound to [your] praise and glory and honor when Jesus Christ (the Messiah, the Anointed One) is revealed."*[56] *"Beloved, do not be amazed and bewildered at the fiery ordeal which is taking place to test your quality, as though something strange (unusual and alien to you and your position) were befalling you."*[57]

God will test your faithfulness in the little things before entrusting you with greater things.[58] He will test your resolve to resist inferior counterfeit offers before blessing you far above all you would dare ask or dream.[59] This means death to your dreams and death to your flesh, to the extent that God becomes a far greater delight to you than any thing or aspiration. When you pass such tests you are proved ready to keep your heart pure and devoted to God in dependence, despite receiving great and abundant blessings. The following two

---

[56] 1 Peter 1:6-8 [57] 1 Peter 4:12 [58] Luke 16:10 [59] Ephesians 3:20

verses sum it all up… *"Delight yourself also in the Lord, and He will give you the desires and secret petitions of your heart."*[60] *"But seek (aim at and strive after) first of all His kingdom and His righteousness (His way of doing and being right), and then all these things taken together will be given you besides."*[61]

And here is the point… *"[That you may really come] to know [practically, through experience for yourselves] the love of Christ, which far surpasses mere knowledge [without experience]; that you may be filled [through all your being] unto all the fullness of God [may have the richest measure of the divine Presence, and become a body wholly filled and flooded with God Himself]!"*[62]

MY TESTIMONY

My flesh has been my greatest enemy against my spiritual empowerment and progression, due to my lack of mastering its desires. For years I lived with a frustrating tension between embracing the promises of God and failing to receive, despite trying really hard. To my grief, after years of striving and striving, I lost all I had seemingly gained; my savings, home, business and even a baby. I realize now I had been living with the wrong emphasis. I had been striving to live a blessed life rather than striving to enter God's rest, who would, if I gave Him a chance, abundantly bless my life. When I began *reading to feed* in 2011 I was so discouraged with Christianity and ready to just give up and walk away.

Early in my Christian life, I caught on to the 'word of faith' and prosperity teaching and my flesh loved it. Hearing that God promises to abundantly bless and favor me was indeed good news and I started to dream big in God. However, after years of praying, believing, giving and waiting, I was still living from hand to mouth. I was confused that the 'big dreams' I was praying for were not materializing. So in time I got frustrated with the fruitlessness of

---

[60] Psalm 37:4 [61] Matthew 6:33 [62] Ephesians 3:19

simply praying and believing, and started to make things happen myself. We bought our own home and business, and success came easily; all was looking good. Although I thought I had entered into blessing, I had actually entered into testing. The little success and recognition that I was enjoying would soon reveal my lack of readiness for God's true abundant blessings.

Very quickly, pride reared its ugly head in me. As far as I was concerned I was moving forward, God was on my side and I was the next 'Donald Trump'. After my wonderful season in 1996 of enjoying intimacy with God through reading my Bible, I traded my Bible for 'Business and Success' biographies. In my heart I vowed to become just as rich and successful; all for the 'glory of God' of course!

We borrowed against the equity in our home and bought a nursery, which Richard and I transformed to achieve 'outstanding status', placing it in the top 1% in the country, with a prestigious award celebration in London. As a result, I started working as a consultant while still owning my nursery. Then to top it all off, I was finally pregnant after trying for years. But within a matter of weeks, I experienced opposition to my nursery from mothers in the local community, lost my baby and fell out with my client that provided me with very lucrative and enjoyable consultancy work. I spiraled into turmoil and wanted to run away from it all. So I sold my nursery (for a good profit) and ventured into recruitment. However, I was not emotionally strong enough to take on a new and unknown business and I certainly was not emotionally strong enough to manage a sales team. Within a matter of months I lost every penny and accrued debts.

But in it all God was so good. We needed to exit from the recruitment business quickly as we had no more money to run it, but exiting would have cost about £25,000. Graciously and lovingly, God provided a buyer who took over the business with all its financial liabilities, so that Richard and I could simply walk away.

Then I finally had my miracle baby and then another, which blessed Richard and me immensely. We also managed to reduce our mortgage payments, and I had maternity benefit payments, which provided for our essential bills. However, our business debt repayments were making things very tight. So after much prayer we sold our home, moved into rented accommodation and paid off our debts.

God blessed us with a lovely home to rent and brought favor so that I could set up a soft play business/ministry in my church, which seemed to be the beginning of our recovery. That is, until He invited us to then give it away.

So where am I now? In a word, thankful! So thankful that I truly know the destructiveness of pride, understand my need to *read to feed* and that I am now living with an increasingly eternal and spiritual perspective. As God promotes me, I rely on the Holy Spirit to guide and empower me to humble myself. I know from personal experience that, promotion without the narrowing and pruning inevitably leads to greater loss and pain. Which I never want to experience ever again.

My experiences and time with God teach me that I am continually a moment from my flesh rising up and making me vulnerable to the sin that crouches at the door of my heart. So I willingly embrace my responsibility to master and crucify my flesh.

When I began *reading to feed* the first time, I experienced deep healing, but as I have said, the second time of *reading to feed* was full of (healing) conviction. The Holy Spirit showed me things about myself that I could never have received from any person. He did it all with such love and encouragement that I felt secure to submit and die to myself.

I want to say yes to my spirit and the Holy Spirit in all things, but inevitably I do not. In the past I excused myself for neglecting God by saying, "Well, God knows my heart." However, God excused King

[63] Acts 13:22 [64] Revelation 2:4

David in this way because he was *"a man after God's own heart."*[63] Such an excuse is only valid for me if my heart is after God with the same intensity and devotion. I am thrilled to say that at last my heart is after God more than it has ever been. I am only scratching the surface of my relationship with Him, and I pray it will continue to increase above all other possible loves. God does not ask to be our only love, but He does insist on being our first love![64]

ACTION STEPS

✦ Love, enjoy, cherish and care for your flesh; it is a precious gift from God.

✦ Love, enjoy, cherish and care for your spirit even more; it is the real, eternal you.

✦ Nourish your spirit so that it can rise above your flesh and empower you in mastering your flesh.

✦ Resist any risings of your flesh, no matter how subtle (as it can be very subtle).

✦ Recognize frustrations regarding purpose, career and ministry as uncircumcised ambition.

✦ Dare to wait and resist pushing doors of opportunity, trusting that God will open doors when you are truly ready.

✦ Dare to make little of your personal spiritual breakthroughs and progress, trusting that God will make much of them.

- Resist waiting and hiding away as a form of penance, but rather as a blissful time of just you and God before you face the trials of God's promotion.

- Be honest with yourself and God regarding the state of your flesh.

PRAYER

Father God, I thank You for this wonderful precious gift of flesh. Thank You that it enables me to function in and enjoy this world, and be a temple to host Your glorious presence. I repent for not managing and mastering my flesh sufficiently and for allowing it to rise up and lead me in living. Please forgive me for allowing my flesh to lead me away from You and Your very best for me. Help me, Father God, to become a master in mastering my flesh and to use it for Your glory. Amen.

PERSONAL COMMITMENT

Realizing that my flesh is not 'me' but that it is 'mine', I will take my responsibility to master it seriously. I will start honestly examining my flesh in the light of God's Word, in prayer and under the Holy Spirit's tuition. Then I commit to accept what I see without excuses and submit to the Holy Spirit's narrowing and pruning. Finally, as my flesh is not 'me' but is 'mine', I will not accept any condemnation but rather embrace conviction from the Holy Spirit as a glorious call to 'come up higher'. A call that I am empowered by grace to accept.

In light of this realization, I will…

....
....
....
....
....
....
....
....

Powerful
Father God,
I surrender to your
superabundant ways
that are far above all I dare ask
or think, beyond my highest
prayers, desires,
thoughts, hopes,
or dreams.

Adapted from Ephesians 3:20 Amplified Bible

SEVEN

LIVING OUT YOUR PURPOSE

BRINGING FORTH YOUR GOLD, TIME TO SHINE!

God lovingly says to you, *"For I know the thoughts and plans that I have for you."*[1] You are born to live a fruitful life that glorifies God and extends His kingdom on this earth!

But how that looks for each person is different. God has deposited gold in you that He desires to refine and put on display; to show off His love and power to your world and beyond. Much frustration comes from having a sense of this gold within, but struggling to know what it is and how to bring it forth. This is because it is not your responsibility to discover or bring forth your gold. It is God's responsibility and desire to reveal it and call it out, while you abide and courageously obey. The teaching in this book is fundamentally about abiding and obeying as a premise to bearing fruit as expressed by Jesus.[2] *"Dwell in Me, and I will dwell in you. [Live in Me, and I will live in you.] Just as no branch can bear fruit of itself without abiding in (being vitally united to) the vine, neither can you bear fruit unless you abide in Me. I am the Vine; you are the branches. Whoever lives in Me and I in him bears much (abundant) fruit. However, apart from Me [cut off from vital union with Me] you can do nothing."*[3]

[1] Jeremiah 29:11 [2] 1 Galatians 5:22 [3] John 15:4-4

IT REALLY IS VERY SIMPLE

In its simplest form, it is easier than we think to be a fruitful Christian; just abide and you will bear fruit... in season.

- ✦ Nourish your spirit so that it can rise up within you and connect with the Holy Spirit.
- ✦ Receive and obey all that flows into your life from your connection.
- ✦ Maintain your connection by continual nourishing and nurturing.
- ✦ Flourish!

Striving to bring God's (or your own) plans to pass leads you away from God, therefore severing your connection. While striving to enter God's rest [4] leads you to God, therefore strengthening your connection.

IT BECOMES VERY COMPLICATED

Natural thinking believes that things happen when we make them happen. It is inconceivable to the flesh that resting in God could be productive and profitable for all areas of our lives. However, God's ways and thoughts are so different from our own, as God spoke through Isaiah, *"For My thoughts are not your thoughts, neither are your ways My ways, says the Lord. For as the heavens are higher than the earth, so are My ways higher than your ways and My thoughts than your thoughts."* [5] Our thoughts and ways are so opposed to God's ways that the expanse of heaven is like the expanse between our ways. Trying to bring to pass God's best with your own reasoning and strength creates a tension that restricts your progress and causes frustration.

God's desire and heart cry is, *"Oh, that My people would listen to Me... would walk in My ways!"* [6] While so often our desire and heart's cry is 'Oh that my God would listen to me, and walk in my ways (bring to pass my heart's desires)!'

---

[4] Hebrews 4:11 [5] Isaiah 55:8-9 [6] Psalm 81:13

God lovingly watches you and says to you, *"Let be and be still, and know (recognize and understand) that I am God. I will be exalted…"*[7] Your ability to bring about God's miraculous plan for your life is nil. Just the same as when Jesus was on this earth, apart from the Father, you can do nothing (of eternal worth). Jesus made this reality very clear… *"I am able to do nothing from Myself [independently, of My own accord—but only as I am taught by God and as I get His orders]. Even as I hear, I judge [I decide as I am bidden to decide. As the voice comes to Me, so I give a decision], and My judgment is right (just, righteous), because I do not seek or consult My own will [I have no desire to do what is pleasing to Myself, My own aim, My own purpose] but only the will and pleasure of the Father Who sent Me."*[8]

This passage gives such clear and powerful keys to living the abundant life. Jesus laid down His own agenda, independence and opinions to simply hear and obey. He lived in a state of being still to know God and see Him exalted in the situations that He faced. Your access to God's resources is dependent on your level of surrender to Him. Develop your relationship with God. Position yourself to hear His voice, know His heart and then you will be trusted with great power and provision.[9] In every situation that you face, revelation is your greatest need. To hear what the Father is saying and see what He is doing will elevate your perspective, from what you can do, to what God can do for and through you.

Surrendering your own agenda, independence and opinions to God can be scary. It can feel as though you are losing control or going backwards. Then when God doesn't do what you think He should within the time frame that you can cope with, you begin questioning, despairing and taking back control, which will suspend or even reverse your progress.

Consider this well-known 'faith analogy': a person is hanging from a ledge, at a great height. As they hang, a voice says, "Let go." The person says, "I can't, it is a long drop… I am scared." The exchange

---

[7] Psalm 46:10 [8] John 5:29-31 [9] Revelation 1:8

goes on like this for some time, and then the person dares to let go. As they begin to fall, they quickly land on a ledge that was just below their feet. To their great relief the provision was closer than they thought.

However, surrendering and obeying isn't always like this. When Richard and I gave away our business, I imagined myself stepping into the scenario above. However, the Holy Spirit showed me a different picture. By giving away our business, we threw ourselves from the ledge out into the air. Then we began to free fall for what seemed like a very short time, and then we caught the updraft of the Holy Spirit and started to soar. In my mind the free falling seemed like a very short time, but in reality the free fall is lasting much longer than I thought I could have coped with. As each month passes by, we just make it financially. However, considering that all our money is gone by the 10th of each month, just making it through the month without accumulating debt is a miracle!

Your faith in God is the most precious thing that God wants to develop in you, and that takes time, trials and testing. Because nothing shall be impossible to him who truly believes in God, His ways and His purposes.[10]

In my season of striving, desperate for breakthrough, I would say to myself, "I know the Bible says, *"Seek first the kingdom and all these things will be added to me,"*[11] but I don't have time to 'just' seek God. My needs are too pressing; I have got to pray, declare, decree and push doors of opportunity. I am merely surviving while I want to be thriving!"

For years, God has been trying to bring me to the point of dependence upon Him in my finances. However, each time He stripped me back, I quickly found my own solution to ease the discomfort. Now I understand that in this present trial I am proving my faith, to develop my endurance, steadfastness and patience by submitting to a thorough work; so that I will *"be perfectly and fully developed [with no defects], lacking in nothing."*[12]

When you are facing desperate need or harboring great dreams, it

---

[10] Matthew 17:20 [11] Matthew 6:33 [12] James 1:2-4

is very scary to just let go. Stopping the striving in prayer and action may feel wrong, counterproductive and a waste of valuable time. However, when you switch from seeking solutions to seeking God, it will be the best thing that you do, and your fastest way forward.

It takes real faith to say to God, "I am going to leave my pressing needs and my desires in your care while I slow down to get to know your voice and ways. I will walk this out more obediently and empowered." Slowing down seems like a backward step; however, it is your fastest way forward. Until you submit to God's first commandment to *"Love the Lord your God with all your heart and with all your soul and with all your mind (intellect)"*,[13] you will only be a shadow of what God has made you to be.

Let God draw you away, to probe your deepest recesses, in a season of suspension and hiding away. Let His eyes spot your depths of rich treasure to mine and refine, to cause it to shine forth from within you. Let your dross be replaced by glorious flecks of gold, sapphire and many precious things, to the glory of God and benefit of humanity, as Job fully understood. *"Surely there is a mine for silver and a place where gold is refined. Iron is taken from the ground, and copper is smelted from ore. A miner puts an end to the darkness; he probes the deepest recesses for ore in the gloomy darkness. He cuts a shaft far from human habitation, in places unknown to those who walk above ground. Suspended far away from people, the miners swing back and forth. Food may come from the earth, but below the surface the earth is transformed as by fire. Its rocks are a source of sapphire, containing flecks of gold. No bird of prey knows that path; no falcon's eye has seen it. Proud beasts have never walked on it; no lion has ever prowled over it. The miner strikes the flint and transforms the mountains at their foundations. He cuts out channels in the rocks, and his eyes spot every treasure. He dams up the streams from flowing so that he may bring light to what is hidden."*[14]

[13] Matthew 22:37 [14] Job 28:1-11

MY TESTIMONY

I never thought 'stopping and surrendering' would be such a productive step. I have spent years striving and striving to achieve and gain, and for a while all the activity seemed to be working. However, because I had not been prepared by God, I was not ready for success and I was never satisfied.

For years I sensed that there was a preacher and biblical teacher within me, I sensed that I would write a book, I sensed that I would be in church leadership and I sensed that I would be a woman who lived by faith—well.

So for years I lived with these things in my heart and mind, trying to find God in it all and trying to 'follow the correct steps' to see all these things come to pass.

Richard and I...

+ Prayed fervently and very regularly. We spent many evenings praying and declaring to enforce our desired victories, because the violent take their victories by force.[15]

+ Listened to faith teaching and preaching. We listened and listened, because faith comes by hearing and hearing by the Word of God.[16]

+ Tithed. Every month (almost), even if it meant we would have to put food on the credit card or were in debt, because we didn't want our finances to be cursed.[17]

+ Gave offerings. We gave over and above our tithe, because tithing opens the windows of heaven and offerings determine how much comes out.[18]

+ Served in church. We attended the meetings and served the Pastor's vision (unquestioningly) because we hoped that as we faithfully served the Pastor's vision, we would in time be promoted.[19]

[15] Matthew 11:12 [16] Romans 10:17 [17] Malachi 3:11 [18] Malachi 3:10 and Luke 6:38 [19] 2 Kings 2:1

However, after fifteen years of such commitment, we were no further forwards. We were financially weak, without any meaningful role in the church, I had not written a book and I had not been given any opportunities to preach and teach what was in my heart.

When I began *reading to feed,* I hid away with God; I stopped all of the striving listed above, and accepted an invitation to start afresh with God. I laid it all down to simply read my Bible, worship God and learn of the Holy Spirit; to learn how to nurture my spiritual vitality and live a kingdom life, i.e. how to pray, give financially and serve the kingdom (in and out of the church). I had to learn (and am still learning) how to do it all as unto the Lord, rather than as unto man and myself.

While I was hiding away in my study undergoing intensive refining, God was actively working on my life. Within two years I have written this book, begun receiving invitations to preach and teach and started actively serving in church leadership with a fresh mission call. What God has done in two years is truly miraculous and all without any help from me! The Holy Spirit has shown me short, mid and long-term insights to my future in Him. If I continue living in what I have described in this book, it will all come to pass. Let me share with you some details of how He has brought these things to pass.

✦ ***Writing this book:*** When I read my Bible cover to cover in 1996, I experienced the power of God's Word but didn't understand it. This time around the Holy Spirit taught me the mechanics behind my experience so that I can maintain it and share it. In the first three months of reading my Bible through, the Holy Spirit taught me from Scripture what He was doing in me with His Word. The teaching in this book is by revelation. I did not set out to study it; the Holy Spirit gave me this understanding as my teacher. As I write this book, I do not refer to any materials, not even my Bible. I simply put down on paper what the Holy Spirit has taught me, drawing on the abundance of God's Word dwelling in me and my testimony. I am uneducated;

I have no formal qualifications or experience for writing this book. If I did not pause and seek God in the way that I have taught you, this book would not exist. There is no way I could have written it. While the content has been easy because it has been given to me, finding the time to write and deciding on a structure has been very hard. This book is a miracle; it is collaboration between the Holy Spirit and myself. He gave me the contents and I have put it down on paper.

✦ ***Preaching and teaching:*** Because of this message that has been formed in me and because of this book, I am receiving invitations to speak. Again, quite simply if I had not paused to seek God, I would not have this message to share. I could have strived to get opportunities to talk and formed interesting messages to share. I could even have 'peddled' my testimony of being an abused child that has known God's healing touch. However, waiting on God has given me something far more powerful, fresh, practical and, therefore, life transforming.

✦ ***Fresh mission call:*** I used to serve in church because of the need for manpower, to gain recognition and to be released into my purpose and calling. Now I serve in and out of church to see Christians experience a revival as I have. I know the hopelessness of spiritual dullness and I sense God's heartbreak over the many who are lukewarm. I serve with a h ope that many more Christians will become revived in spirit and join together in unity to create a widespread revival; a revival that is sustainable because it is based on individuals abiding in God's powerful Word.

✦ ***Friendships:*** Part of my refining was feeling loneliness, intensified in extremely painful ways. God told me that He would build a community around me. This seemed impossible, but He is doing just that. I now have such special kingdom friendships all added by God.

✦ ***Living by faith:*** I had resisted the pruning of greed and financial idolatry from my heart, but now I embrace it. Each month is a miracle as we see God provide and avoid accumulating debt.

It hasn't been easy and we have had to take some hard, radical and costly steps. There have been occasions when I have wanted to get a job to escape the tests and trials of financial lack. One day I sat at my computer in floods of tears, staring at a job advert. The job was within my professional comfort zone, tempting me with funded relocation back to my home town and an unusually generous salary for the role. While sobbing I told Richard, "I am applying for this job" to which he replied, "Lets pray about it." After a few days of intentionally waiting on God, I heard very clearly that applying for the job would suspend our current kingdom journey. So in faith I did not apply for the job. Although it can be very challenging and at times scary, I would not have it any other way. I have only just scratched the surface of who God is and what I can be in Him. I have my down days for sure, but my sense of what God is doing keeps me going.

MAINTENANCE

I have managed to maintain reading to feed since I began, but the intensity changes with varying seasons. After many months of rising very early, my squeaky stairs began to make it impossible, as my son became sensitive to their sound in his sleep. I would try skipping steps and creeping gingerly, but every time my son would be woken up and want to join me. Then my children stopped napping in the day time and all the precious time that I had fought for was slipping away. So I had to carve out new times and ways. When it became really hard to find the length of time that I desired each day, I did what I could without any condemnation, but longed for more. My prayer was, 'Father, set up my life so that when my children's time in education increases I can stay home with you, rather than getting a job.' I could pray this prayer because I had paid the price to carve out time when it seemed impossible. I am now entering a wonderful season, where I have two hours child free each weekday, which are for God and me. In addition to this, Richard and I are making extra time in the mornings and evenings because we are so hungry. Life will always come against making the time to read to feed and fellowship with God. However, once you have experienced the goodness of reading to feed you will have desire to motivate you. In all the seasons, watch your desire; what you desire and yearn to spend your time on will indicate your spiritual health. In all of the seasons fight to maintain a basic reading to feed commitment. Then push yourself to go for more. Be greedy for time with God, passionately pursuing all that you can enjoy. Continually evaluate your life honestly before God. Never accept condemnation for what you aren't doing, and yet, never be satisfied with what you are doing.

Whatever you face and whatever you desire, dare to step off the treadmill and learn to walk it out with God. He will bring great things to pass in ways that are so contrary to your own ways, but so much better. Glory to God!

ACTION STEPS

+ Build up your spirit, maintain *reading to feed*. If you stop, don't worry; just start again.

+ Renew your mind, take what you read personally and allow yourself to be influenced and challenged.

+ Let your heart be circumcised; repent of anything that the Holy Spirit raises to deal with. Don't resist Him by making excuses or burying it; rather seek and accept conviction as a glorious call higher.

+ Master your flesh; your flesh is not you, it is yours. So build up the true eternal you, the spirit you, to lead your soul in mastering your flesh.

- Arise, Shine! God will do amazing things with your life. It will be challenging and costly at times, but so worth it!

- Maintain an eternal perspective; whatever God takes you through is for your eternal good. Pass the tests and enjoy the amazing rewards.

- Seek first God, delight yourself in Him and trust that He will add to your life and give you the desires and secret petitions of your heart. Guaranteed!

PRAYER

Father God, I dare to lay it all down. I dare to stop striving and start abiding. Help me to know what I should lay down and help me to abide. Grant me the revelations that I need to do this for the rest of my life. Whenever I get back into striving, please tell me and draw me back into resting in You. Give me grace to walk out my life in obedience to Your higher ways and go the distance with You. Amen.

COMMITMENT

Now I see that the way to go forward in life is to retreat into You, I commit to…

....
....
....
....
....
....
....
....

My first revival Bible, so precious to me.

CONCLUSION

It has been an honor to share my journey in this book; thank you for taking the time to read it.

Now it is over to you to go on your own epic journey with God. Simply read your Bible to know God and let the Holy Spirit lead you in the rest. Above all, go at your own pace, be consistent and enjoy the connections.

I pray that the impact my teaching and testimony has made in your heart will take root and multiply. I know that the Holy Spirit will bring about a great harvest in and through you.

"And now [brethren], I commit you to God [I deposit you in His charge, entrusting you to His protection and care]. And I commend you to the Word of His grace [to the commands and counsels and promises of His unmerited favor]. It is able to build you up and to give you [your rightful] inheritance among all God's set-apart ones (those consecrated, purified, and transformed of soul)." Acts 20:32

How did you get on? Do you have any questions?
Email me at kim@ReadYourBibleForRevival.org
or visit www.ReadYourBibleForRevival.org

Kim

Made in the USA
Charleston, SC
18 November 2013